G000093109

Sister Stanislaus Kennedy is an [?] the founder of Focus Ireland, the Inaugural Council of Young Social Innovation, Ireland, and the Sanctuary. She has been instrumental in developing and implementing social-service programmes that have benefited thousands of people in need throughout Ireland and Europe. For this work, she has received many awards, including Honorary Degrees of Law from Trinity College Dublin, the National University of Ireland and the Open University, as well as a presidential medal from New York University.

She has written four bestselling books, *Now is the Time*, *Gardening the Soul*, *Seasons of the Day* and *Stillness Through My Prayers*, and is currently working on her latest book.

www.transworldireland.ie

www.**rbooks**.co.uk

Also by Sister Stan

GARDENING THE SOUL
NOW IS THE TIME
STILLNESS THROUGH MY PRAYERS

and published by Transworld Ireland

Seasons of the Day

A Book of Hours

SISTER STAN

TRANSWORLD IRELAND

TRANSWORLD IRELAND
an imprint of The Random House Group Limited
20 Vauxhall Bridge Road, London SW1V 2SA
www.rbooks.co.uk

SEASONS OF THE DAY
A TRANSWORLD IRELAND BOOK: 9781848271647

First published in Great Britain and Ireland by TownHouse, 2003
Transworld Ireland edition published 2009

Printed and bound in Great Britain by Clays Ltd, St Ives PLC

Text design and typeset by Anú Design, Tara.

2 4 6 8 10 9 7 5 3 1

The Random House Group Limited supports The Forest Stewardship
Council (FSC®), the leading international forest certification organisation.
Our books carrying the FSC label are printed on FSC® certified paper.
FSC is the only forest certification scheme endorsed by the leading
environmental organisations, including Greenpeace. Our
paper procurement policy can be found at
www.randomhouse.co.uk/environment

Contents

Acknowledgements

I wish to express my appreciation and gratitude to all at TownHouse who encouraged me to write this book in the first place and continued to support me as I did so. A very special thanks to Siobhán Parkinson for her inspired editorial work and guidance, to Barbara Merriman, who typed different drafts of the book and especially to Síle Wall, who typed and was involved with all of the drafts.

Finally, I would like to thank all those who have been a source of inspiration to me throughout my life and who, in one way or another, are all in this book.

Sr Stanislaus Kennedy
August 2003

Introduction

MATINS	*Pre-dawn*
LAUDS	*Daybreak*
PRIME	*Early morning*
TERCE	*Late morning*
SEXT	*High noon*
NONES	*Afternoon*
VESPERS	*Evening*
COMPLINE	*Nightfall*

This book is a journey through the hours of the monastic day. It is an invitation to hear the sound of silence, to step out of clock time into the monastic flow of time, to stop, to reflect, to listen, to respond and to come to a new understanding of the deep inner peace that silence and true listening can bring. It is an attempt to share with you some of the insights and inspirations I have gained from the canonical hours and I hope this sharing will bring you the joy, consolation and solace present within them and the confidence to use them in your own day.

As the liturgical Book of Hours is a series of psalms, hymns, reflections and prayers arranged to be chanted eight times a day, seven days a week in a four-week cycle, I designed this book in the same way, using short psalm extracts, reflections and prayers. I hope you will make this book your own and use it whatever way best helps you to build into your daily life moments of stillness and silence and to keep in touch with the rhythms and seasons of your heart.

You may, of course, use this book in any way that appeals to you. You may, for example, feel drawn to choose one hour that you will observe every day; or you might decide to choose two hours, one for the morning and the evening; or three, to give your day a beginning, middle and end, using whatever hour is appropriate for the time you have chosen to mark these points in your day. Of course, if your daily routine allows, you may find you can use most, or even all, of the hours each day, even if only for a short period, for example while convalescing or taking a retreat or other break.

Another way you might use this book is to take a line or a verse from any of the hours as a mantra for the day or for the week, so that you can have a chant in your heart every day.

Alternatively, you could choose an hour that suits a particular time of the year – *vespers* in autumn, for example. Or you might find that a particular hour suits a particular season in your own life: thus for example you might choose *matins* at a time when you feel the need to trust the darkness in your life; or *lauds* at a time when you want to give thanks; or *prime* at a time when you need to be more reflective about what you do and how you do it; *terce* as a reminder of the importance of being in tune and connected with the rhythm of your life; *sext* at a time when you feel the need to renew your commitment and dedication; *nones* when you need to remind yourself of the impermanence and the endurance of all things; *vespers* when you want to feel reminded that you are not indispensable but part of the bigger picture; or you may choose *compline* at a time when you feel the need to surrender or to rest.

The Canonical Hours

Every day, all over the world, chants are sung by religious communities during what is known as the eight canonical hours. These hours are public services of praise and worship that take place at appointed times each day. Most of the contemplative orders chant the complete eight hours, while other priests and religious chant or recite parts of it. Some lay people also observe the hours, and one purpose of this book is to help people use these prayers in whatever way suits their lives.

The purpose of the canonical hours is to sanctify the day and all human activity. The different hours mark the different 'seasons' of the day, and the pattern of the hours was designed to fit in with the natural rhythm of the day.

Hours as Seasons

The special liturgical and monastic meaning of the word 'hour' goes back to the Greek word *hora*, which is older than our notion of a day consisting of twenty-four sixty-minute periods. The original religious notion of the hour is not so much a numerical measure of time but a soul measure.

We can come to an appreciation of what an 'hour' originally meant if we reflect on the seasons of the year. Whatever our diary might tell us, seasons do not start on particular dates. Seasons are qualitative experiences, rather than calendar periods. We sense subtle difference in the quality of light, the length of the day, something in the air. We notice a change in nature, and we say that a particular season is upon the earth.

The hours are the seasons of the day. Earlier generations, which were not ruled by alarm clocks or calendars, saw the hours as the way the day naturally ebbed and flowed through shades of light and darkness, as the day began, grew, blossomed, bore fruit and receded, with the same rhythm as everything that grows and changes on the earth.

Each hour has a character more complex than our sterile clock time. An hour, in this sense, is more a mood than a measurement of time. Although the word 'canonical', which is applied to the hours in the monastic tradition, originally meant a measuring rod, the hours are a way of measuring the day by its different moods rather than by any strict measure of time.

The hours provide a framework or a structure by which the monastic day is supported. They are the inner structure for living consciously and responsibly through the stages of the day. The monastic relationship to time through the canonical hours is seen as a way to sensitise the monks and nuns who chant them to the nuances of time. The hours signify a very different relationship with time from the one we have grown used to. The singing of the canonical hours helps the monks and nuns to find and experience a sense of the *now* which so often eludes us.

From the monastic perspective, time is a series of opportunities and encounters. When we live in the *now*, we attune ourselves to the call of each moment, listening and responding to what each hour, each situation brings. This is very different from how most of us live our busy lives today, barely noticing the different qualities and characters of the stages of the day – pre-dawn, daybreak, early morning, late morning, high noon, afternoon, evening, nightfall. Saturated with information, our day is deprived of meaning and we are caught in a never-ending swirl of duties and demands, things to finish and things to put right.

And yet we sense that there is more to life than this. Our uneasiness is caused by our distorted sense of time – which we are always running out of. The liturgy of the hours shows us that there is another way to live in this noisy, distracted world of ours and that this way is not as far out of our reach as we think. The liturgy of the hours speaks to our hearts because it is a universal call to enter the *now*, a call to stop, to listen, to hear the message of this moment. The liturgy of the hours can speak to the contemplative in each of us. It speaks to our souls, which long for peace and connection to an ultimate source of meaning and value. It calls us to live in the present and puts us in touch with the rhythm of life, the rhythm of the universe. It helps us to become still, and reminds us to live lives that are directed by the spirit within us. It reminds us to live intentionally, responding to what life brings us and not to be swept away by endless timetables, deadlines and agendas. It reminds us that, although time is a precious commodity, it isn't as scarce as many of us believe. Above all, the liturgy of the hours teaches us that life is meant to be joyful. When we chant the hours, we experience a deep joy that comes from within, from our own hearts. The meaning and character of each of the hours is outlined below.

Hour by Hour, Through the Day

MATINS   *Pre-dawn – Silent waiting*
I have only participated very occasionally in *matins* at a monastery, but it was always an awe-inspiring experience. There is something so pure about *matins*. It has no purpose but God alone, for there is only the darkness, the silence and the chant. At *matins*, you can get this extraordinary feeling of being caught up in mystery, wrapped in the divine. The night watch is a reminder of the deeper mystery of our lives.

LAUDS   *Daybreak – Thanksgiving*
Lauds takes us from darkness into light, a time to delight in the new sunrise, a time to give thanks for the gift of the new day, the new moment, a reminder that every new day is a gift not merited and that our natural response is gratitude. It is a reminder that we can take nothing for granted; that once we do take things for granted, we lose our sense of surprise and our delight in the gift and the giver. The chant of *lauds* is extra joyful, full of praise to

God for a world reborn each day. The monastic experience of greeting the new day with joy, gratitude and surprise can be our experience too, if we choose to be attentive to the dawn.

PRIME

Early morning – Work

At *prime*, the monks and nuns move into the work of the day. In some monasteries, work duties are allocated at *prime*. It is the time to remind ourselves of good beginnings, of blessings and reflecting on what we do. It is a reminder of the importance of generosity and a whole-hearted giving to work. It is a reminder of the sacredness of all things, a time to savour the dignity of work, a time to offer ourselves to God as co-creators of the world. *Prime* is a reminder of the importance of clarifying and purifying our intentions, our plans, priorities and values, a time to be open to the challenges and opportunities of the new day, a time to recognise our interconnectedness with all creation; a call to work now and to sow seeds, the fruits of which we may never see.

TERCE

Late morning – Blessing

Terce is a time of blessing. This is the fourth hour in the day. In monastic life, the Holy Spirit is invoked to bless the works of the day. *Terce* is a reminder that the work is God's and that we all share in God's life and it is God who gives the increase through us. The more alive we are with the life of God, the more blessed we are and the more blessings flow from us. It is also a reminder of the original blessing of life that is a pure gift. *Terce* reminds us to tune into the rhythms of life and the rhythms of the cosmos, to be open to the wonder and bounty of life.

SEXT

High noon – Renewal

Sext is the hour of fervour, a time for the monks and nuns to renew their commitment and enthusiasm and a time to restore life. At noon, the sun shines at its fullest, but it is also a time of great silence in nature. It is a time when nature rests, and so too monks and nuns stop to renew their dedication and to refresh themselves physically through their midday meal, which is their main meal. It is the monastic life in tune with the turning point of the day, a time for renewal and reflection. Reflection at midday is a deliberate, conscious act, a reminder to ask for the grace to continue.

In the monastic life, as monks and nuns celebrate their main meal, they also celebrate and renew themselves in their service of each other as they take turns to serve the meal. We too can renew ourselves through refreshing ourselves physically, through reminding ourselves of the importance of the people around us, for example our work colleagues, and through remembering our place in the world before our creator.

NONES   *Afternoon – Forgiveness*

Nones is the hour of the mid to late afternoon and a reminder of the impermanence of all things and, at the same time, the endurance of all things. It is a time to be conscious – conscious of our aloneness, of our mortality, of forgiveness, of giving up, of a right understanding of our limits. Day began in darkness with the light breaking through, reaching its peak at noon, and now the light begins to decline. The chant associated with *nones* has a serenity about it. It is a recognition that the day is declining, the evening is approaching and the enthusiasm of the earlier part of the day gives way to serenity.

VESPERS   *Evening – Relinquishing*

Vespers celebrates the descent of evening and the lighting of the lamps. At this time, the daylight fades away and silence descends on the earth. Monastic life follows this rhythm of the earth and the monks and nuns leave their work and prepare to solemnly chant *vespers*, to celebrate the day and the sunset. The chanting of *vespers* reminds us that we are not indispensable, we can all be done without. We are one part of the bigger picture, the bigger world of God, but we can withdraw from that at times and it carries on beautifully and wonderfully without us.

COMPLINE   *Nightfall – Vigilance*

Compline is the conclusion of the monastic day. It is about closure and about being vigilant, confronting our fears with faith and trust. It is about returning home, it is about blessing. Night is a time for questions: Am I safe? Am I loved? It is the time when the monks and nuns examine their conscience and ask for forgiveness of God and of each other before going to sleep.

Night is a time to be receptive, a time to listen, to wait, to reflect and to think things over, to sleep on things before making judgements and commitments. At *compline*, we place ourselves under the protection of God, and face up, with faith and trust, to our fears of night and death. The poet Rilke writes about *compline*: 'I am returning home out of my wings in which I lost myself.'

Originally *compline* was not part of the hours, which formerly finished with *vespers*. *Compline* was a later addition, which was said in the cloisters and not in the oratories as it is said now.

This book is an attempt to preserve and hand on the spirit and values of a culture and a way of life that is rooted in the earth and touches the sky.

The Hours of the Day

MATINS   Pre-dawn

LAUDS   Daybreak

PRIME   Early morning

TERCE   Late morning

SEXT   High noon

NONES   Afternoon

VESPERS   Evening

COMPLINE   Nightfall

Week One

OUR WORD IS a lamp for my steps
and a light for my path.
I have sworn and have made up my
mind to obey your decrees.
Your will is my heritage for ever,
the joy of my heart.
I set myself to carry out your statutes
in fullness, for ever.

Psalm (118) 119: 105–106, 111–112

Matins
opening to God's prompting within
an act of faith

Faith
the eternal yes
to God
to life

defining us
opening our lives
to all that is
creative
beautiful
challenging
loving

offering
new insights
different perspectives

calling us to
hear a deeper reality

Your word is a lamp for my steps and a light for my path.

HE LORD IS my light and my help;
whom shall I fear?
The Lord is the stronghold of my life;
before whom shall I shrink?

When evildoers draw near
to devour my flesh,
it is they, my enemies and foes,
who stumble and fall.

Though an army encamp against me
my heart would not fear.
Though war break out against me
even then would I trust.

Psalm (26) 27: 1–3

Each dawn
a genesis
a new beginning
a resurrection
a promise
moving out of darkness
into light

a time
to rejoice
a moment
neither dark nor light

a time
to delight

in light
determined to come

a time
to give thanks
for the gift of life

a time
to reach out
receive this day
with joy

The Lord is my light and my help.

IT IS YOU, O Lord, who are my hope,
my trust, O Lord, since my youth.
On you I have leaned from my birth;
from my mother's womb you have been my help.
My hope has always been in you.

My fate has filled many with awe
but you are my strong refuge.
My lips are filled with your praise,
with your glory all the day long.
Do not reject me now that I am old;
when my strength fails do not forsake me.

Psalm (70) 71: 5–9

*Morning
the womb of life*

*pregnant with
courage
challenge
goodness
seeds of new beginnings*

On you I have leaned from my birth.

SRAEL! BLESS THE Lord:
give glory and eternal praise to him.
Priests! bless the Lord:
give glory and eternal praise to him.
Servants of the Lord! bless the Lord:
give glory and eternal praise to him.
Spirits and souls of the virtuous! bless the Lord.

Canticle of Daniel 3: 83–87

Pausing
at terce

Blessing with
a word
a smile
a kindness
a prayer
our lives are blessed

Blessed
we bless in our turn
in our way
on our way

You, holy and humble of heart, O bless the Lord.

PEN TO ME the gates of holiness:
I will enter and give thanks.
This is the Lord's own gate
where the just may enter.
I will thank you for you have answered
and you are my saviour.

Psalm (117) 118: 19–21

Midday
Angelus bells
prayer time
an ancient Christian tradition
calling us to pray
an ancient monastic call
to pray
in fields
schools
hospitals
towns
offices
homes
factories
shops
cars
buses
trains
planes
on streets

we pause to pray
pray for peace

Open to me the gates of holiness: I will enter and give thanks.

IN YOU, O Lord, I take refuge.
Let me never be put to shame.
In your justice, set me free,
hear me and speedily rescue me.

Be a rock of refuge for me,
a mighty stronghold to save me,
for you are my rock, my stronghold.
For your name's sake, lead me and guide me.

Psalm (30) 31: 2–4

Nones
awareness of the
impermanence
transitoriness
limitations
of the material

Nones
awareness of the
permanence
endurance
timelessness
of the spiritual
the eternal

You are my rock, my stronghold.

WILL HEAR what the Lord has to say,
a voice that speaks of peace,
peace for his people and friends
and those who turn to God in their hearts.
Salvation is near for the God-fearing,
and his glory will dwell in our land.

Mercy and faithfulness have met;
justice and peace have embraced.
Faithfulness shall spring from the earth
and justice look down from heaven.

Psalm (84) 85: 9–12

Sun sets
evening descends
light fades
day draws to a close
lamps are lit

Vespers
a new glow streams across our day
hour of peace
silence falling on the world

Setting aside our day
we enter serenity

I will hear what the Lord has to say.

ORD, YOU ARE my shepherd;
there is nothing I shall want.
Fresh and green are the pastures
where you give me repose.
Near restful waters you lead me,
to revive my drooping spirit.

Psalm (22) 23: 1–3

Receptivity
a condition of the night
a reminder of the often unrecognised virtue
of lives lived in dependency
of lives lived in the service of others

**Near restful waters you lead me, to revive my
drooping spirit.**

I REMEMBER THE days that are past;
I ponder all your works.
I muse on what your hand has wrought
and to you I stretch out my hands.
Like a parched land my soul thirsts for you.

Lord make haste and answer;
for my spirit fails within me.
Do not hide your face
lest I become like those in the grave.

In the morning let me know your love
for I put my trust in you.
Make me know the way I should walk;
to you I lift up my soul.

Psalm (142) 143: 5–8

Opening to our inner selves
quietens our mind from
busyness
noisy mindlessness
prejudices
judgements

Opening to our inner selves
frees us
to trust each new moment
in time

calls us
to attentive listening

invites us to hear
that small voice deep inside
the voice of God

Like a parched land my soul thirsts for you.

THEY ARE HAPPY, whose God is the Lord,
the people who are chosen as his own.
From the heavens the Lord looks forth
and sees all the people of the earth.

From the heavenly dwelling God gazes
on all the dwellers on the earth;
God who shapes the hearts of them all
and considers all their deeds.

Psalm (32) 33: 12–15

February
early morning
little rays of light come seeping in

daybreak
in a Dublin church

Dawn washing through
stained-glass windows
a tapestry of reds, blues, golds

illuminating the glorious ascent into heaven
an invitation to greet this new day
witnessing the risen Christ

God looks forth and sees all the people of the earth.

IN YOU, O Lord, I take refuge;
let me never be put to shame.
In your justice rescue me, free me;
pay heed to me and save me.

Be a rock where I can take refuge,
a mighty stronghold to save me;
for you are my rock, my stronghold.
Free me from the hand of the wicked,
from the grip of the unjust, of the oppressor.

Psalm (70) 71: 1–4

Not knowing

embracing
inevitability

facing the unseen
with courage

freeing us to
look forward
believe in goodness
go forth

to meet
and embrace
each new day

In you, O Lord, I take refuge.

ET THE EARTH bless the Lord,
give glory and eternal praise to him.
Mountains and hills! bless the Lord:
give glory and eternal praise to him.
Every thing that grows on the earth! bless the Lord:
give glory and eternal praise to him.
Springs of water! bless the Lord:
give glory and eternal praise to him.
Seas and rivers! bless the Lord:
give glory and eternal praise to him.
Sea beasts and everything that lives in water!
bless the Lord:
give glory and eternal praise to him.
Birds of heaven! all bless the Lord:
give glory and eternal praise to him.
Animals wild and tame! all bless the Lord:
give glory and eternal praise to him.

Canticle of Daniel 3: 74–82

O breath of God
calling us forth
from the dust of the earth

In your likeness
we are made
dust of your earth
in your breath
made divine

Embracing our dustiness
and breathiness
is holy work

Let the earth bless the Lord.

PRAISE GOD IN his holy place,
Sing praise in the mighty heavens.
Sing praise for God's powerful deeds,
praise God's surpassing greatness.

Sing praise with sound of trumpet,
sing praise with lute and harp.
Sing praise with timbrel and dance,
sing praise with strings and pipes.

Sing praise with resounding cymbals,
sing praise with clashing of cymbals.
Let everything that lives and that breathes
give praise to the Lord.

Psalm 150: 1–6

Stopping
pausing
part of the rhythm
in Buddhist communities

a mindfulness bell is rung
everyone stops
taking three mindful breaths

Bell or no bell
stopping
brings us
to the now of today

Before turning on the computer
opening the door
getting into the car
answering the phone
let us stop, pause and breathe

mindful
still
at peace

Let everything that lives and that breathes give praise.

OW GREAT IS the goodness, Lord,
that you keep for those who fear you,
that you show to those who trust you
in the sight of all.

You hide them in the shelter of your presence
from human plots;
you keep them safe within your tent
from disputing tongues.

Psalm (30) 31: 20–21

Nones
a challenge

Making something of the day
before it is too late
before letting it go

Giving ourselves to the joy of the day
before leaving it

How great is the goodness, Lord.

LORD, YOU once favoured your land
and revived the fortunes of Jacob,
you forgave the guilt of your people
and covered all their sins.
You averted all your rage,
you calmed the heart of your anger.

Psalm (84) 85: 2–4

Vespers
resting in the peace of evening
conflicts and contradictions
are healed
resolved

Reflecting on the
brokenness and fragility of
our day
our world
we go forward in a spirit of quiet festivity
greeting the silence of descending dark

You forgave the guilt of your people.

I F I SHOULD walk in the valley of
darkness
no evil would I fear.
You are there with your crook
and your staff;
with these you give me comfort.

Psalm (22) 23: 4

Night-time

learning to be present
to the present
in mindfulness
in recollection

letting go of fear
trusting the dark
the beginning of serenity

You give me comfort.

AM HERE and I call, you will hear
me, O God.
Turn your ear to me; hear my words.
Display your great love, you whose right hand saves
your friends from those who rebel against them.

Guard me as the apple of your eye.
Hide me in the shadow of your wings
from the violent attack of the wicked.

Psalm (16) 17: 6–9

Before day breaks upon us
setting aside time
in the silence of meditation
guards us
protects us
enriches us
cultivates attentiveness

boundaries created by our minds
begin to blur and dissolve
bringing peace

Hide me in the shadow of your wings.

N GOD ALONE is my soul at rest;
from God comes my help.
God alone is my rock, my stronghold,
my fortress; I stand firm.

Psalm (61) 62: 2–3

To know the light
we must know the dark

To be full
we must be empty

The darkness of night
pregnant
with new light

Out of darkness
dawn light
creating new life

In God alone is my soul at rest.

LORD, IT is you who are my portion
and my cup,
it is you yourself who are my prize.
The lot marked out for me is my delight,
welcome indeed the heritage that falls to me!

I will bless you, Lord, you give me counsel,
and even at night direct my heart.
I keep you, Lord, ever in my sight;
since you are at my right hand, I shall stand firm.

Psalm (15) 16: 5–8

Prime

time of fortitude
sturdiness
in the face of loss

robustness
in the face of difficulty

tenacity
to begin again
in the face of adversity

endurance
suffused with hope

You are at my right hand, I shall stand firm.

ALL THINGS THE Lord has made, bless the Lord:
give glory and eternal praise to him.
Angels of the Lord! all bless the Lord:
give glory and eternal praise to him.
Heavens! bless the Lord:
give glory and eternal praise to him.
Waters above the heavens! bless the Lord:
give glory and eternal praise to him.
Powers of the Lord! all bless the Lord:
give glory and eternal praise to him.
Sun and moon! bless the Lord:
give glory and eternal praise to him.
Stars of heaven! bless the Lord:
give glory and eternal praise to him.
Showers and dews! all bless the Lord:
give glory and eternal praise to him.

Canticle of Daniel 3: 57–64

Life
God's life
divine vitality in us all

Divine life
given
blessed
expressed
shared
passed on
through our humanity
NOW

Eternal life
in time
out of time
the eternal NOW

To God be highest glory and praise forever.

ES, CHILDREN ARE a gift from the Lord,
a blessing, the fruit of the womb.
The sons and daughters of youth
are like arrows in the hand of a warrior.

O the happiness of those
who have filled their quiver with these arrows!
They will have no cause for shame
when they dispute with their foes in the gateways.

Psalm (126) 127: 3–5

Believing goodness awaits us
we stop—
tasting its gift

Believing creation is flawed
we stop—
feeling the fear

Believing our soul is luminous
we stop—
discovering life's blessings

**Children are a gift from the Lord, a blessing, the
fruit of the womb.**

AT EPHRATA WE heard of the ark;
we found it in the plains of Yearim.
'Let us go the place of his dwelling;
let us go to kneel at God's footstool.'

Go up, Lord, to the place of your rest,
you and the ark of your strength.

Psalm (131) 132: 6–8

Mortality
reminding us
to do
what we do
well
happily
joyfully
freely

reminding us
to live in the now

Let us go the place of his dwelling; let us go to
kneel at his footstool.

LESS THE LORD, my soul!
Lord God, how great you are,
clothed in majesty and glory,
wrapped in light as in a robe!

The trees of the Lord drink their fill,
the cedars God planted on Lebanon;
there the birds build their nests;
on the treetop the stork has her home.
The goats find a home on the mountains
and rabbits hide in the rocks.

You made the moon to mark the months;
the sun knows the time for its setting.
When you spread the darkness it is night
and all the beasts of the forest creep forth.
The young lions roar for their prey
and ask their food from God.

Psalm (103) 104: 1–2, 16–21

In the cool of the evening
God walked with Adam and Eve
in the Garden of Eden

In the cool of the evening
the dove returned to Noah
with the olive branch in its beak

In the cool of the evening
Jesus was laid in the tomb

after three days
he rose again

In the cool of the evening
we reflect
on the gifts of the parting day

You made the moon to mark the months; the sun
knows the time for its setting.

IKE THE DEER that yearns
for running streams,
so my soul is yearning
for you, my God.

My soul is thirsting for God,
the God of my life;
when can I enter and see
the face of God?

My tears have become my bread,
by night, by day,
as I hear it said all the day long:
'Where is your God?'

Psalm (41) 42: 2–4

Learning
in the quiet of night
to listen
to our own silence
the unaccepted parts of ourselves
the silences around us
the silence of those in pain
the silence of children
the silence of oppressed people
who dare not speak

Learning
to listen to
systems

cultures
customs
that reinforce troubled silences

Learning
to listen to
the silence of
earth
air
water
fire

Learning
to move
into the centre of all silence
where the spirit dwells

My soul is yearning for you, my God.

THERE IS ONE thing I ask of the Lord,
for this I long,
to live in the house of the Lord,
all the days of my life,
to savour the sweetness of the Lord,
to behold his temple.

For the Lord makes me safe in his tent
in the day of evil.
God hides me in the shelter of his tent,
on a rock I am secure.

Psalm (26) 27: 4–5

Vigil
calling us to
savour that gentle presence within

reminding us to
bring a sense of the sacred into the day
carry it like a song in our heart

permeating
everything we do
everything we say
everything we are
with sacredness
with holiness

God hides me in the shelter of his tent.

O MY WORDS give ear, O Lord,
give heed to my groaning.
Attend to the sound of my cries,
my king and my God.

It is you whom I invoke, O Lord.
In the morning you hear me;
in the morning I offer you my prayer,
watching and waiting.

Psalm 5: 2–4

Watching
the last darkness
of night sky dissipate

Waiting
as the sun filters through

another miracle
day starting
before day breaks

A chance
to stop
wait
watch
give thanks

a new day, a new gift

**In the morning I offer you my prayer, watching
and waiting.**

OR YOUR LOVE is better than life,
my lips will speak your praise.
So I will bless you all my life,
in your name I will lift up my hands.
My soul shall be filled as with a banquet,
my mouth shall praise you with joy.

Psalm (62) 63: 4–6

Stopping at prime
taking a moment to
become conscious of who we are
bringing together the threads of our history

reminding us
where we have come from
remembering
where we are heading
what we are drawn to
why we do what we do

Your love is better than life.

INDS! ALL BLESS the Lord:
give glory and eternal praise to him.
Fire and heat! bless the Lord:
give glory and eternal praise to him.
Cold and heat! bless the Lord:
give glory and eternal praise to him.
Dews and sleets! bless the Lord:
give glory and eternal praise to him.
Frost and cold! bless the Lord:
give glory and eternal praise to him.
Ice and snow! bless the Lord:
give glory and eternal praise to him.
Nights and days! bless the Lord:
give glory and eternal praise to him.
Light and darkness! bless the Lord:
give glory and eternal praise to him.
Lightning and clouds! bless the Lord:
give glory and eternal praise to him.

Canticle of Daniel 3: 65–73

Life
time to bless

Life
puff of winter cold
flash of a swallow
sound of a mosquito
shadow across our path
whispering of wind

scent of hay
cadence of greeting
singing, welcoming
tissue of a rose
last glimmer of daylight
first light of dawn
bud of a snowdrop

Life
blessings from God

Nights and days! Bless the Lord.

T IS GOD the Lord most high
who gives each a place.
In the register of peoples God writes:
'These are her children,'
and while they dance they will sing:
'In you all find their home.'

Psalm (86) 87: 6–7

Sext
turning point
in the day

time of stillness
peace
renewal
restoration
within church
outside church

stillness
present
in any space
every place
available
always
everywhere
to all
who seek it

In you all will find their home.

HE LORD LOOKS on those who fear him,
on those who hope in his love,
to rescue their souls from death,
to keep them alive in famine.

Our soul is waiting for the Lord.
The Lord is our help and our shield.
Our hearts find joy in the Lord.
We trust in God's holy name.

May your love be upon us, O Lord,
as we place all our hope in you.

Psalm (32) 33: 18–22

Day drawing to a close

time
to offer
what we have
undone
done
left undone

time
to let go
relinquish
possession of the day

time
to give back freely
what we have been freely given

Our soul is waiting for the Lord.

PRAISE THE Lord, Jerusalem!
Zion, praise your God!

God has strengthened the bars of your gates,
and has blessed the children within you;
has established peace on your borders,
and feeds you with finest wheat.

God sends out word to the earth
and swiftly runs the command.
God showers down snow white as wool,
and scatters hoarfrost like ashes.

Psalm (147) 147B: 12–16

Nature
harmonious
purposeful
ordered
ebbing
flowing

Day
one pulse in the cycle
of endings and beginnings
sowing and reaping
planting and harvesting
spring and autumn
morning and evening

**God showers down snow white as wool, and
scatters hoarfrost like ashes.**

SAID: 'I will be watchful of my ways
for fear I should sin with my tongue.
I will put a curb on my lips
when the wicked stand before me.'
I was mute, silent and still.
Their prosperity stirred my grief.

My heart was burning within me.
At the thought of it, the fire blazed up
and my tongue burst into speech:
'O Lord, you have shown me my end,
how short is the length of my days.
Now I know how fleeting is my life.'

Psalm (38) 39: 2–5

Attentiveness to what is there
enlarges what is
everything
taking on a new significance
deepening our sense of wonder
as day fades

How short is the length of my days. Now I know
how fleeting is my life.

OR IT WAS you who created my being,
knit me together in my mother's womb.
I thank you for the wonder of my being,
for the wonders of all your creation.

Already you knew my soul,
my body held no secret from you
when I was being fashioned in secret
and moulded in the depths of the earth.

Psalm (138) 139: 13–15

In the night watch
we come to know the
mysteriousness
unnameability
unknowableness
of God

we come to know
that God
cannot be made in our image
according to our way

we come to know
that you, O God
are always shaping us
creating us
in your likeness

It was you who created my being.

OOK TOWARDS GOD and be radiant;
let your faces not be abashed.
When the poor cry out the Lord hears them
and rescues them from all their distress.

The Angel of the Lord is encamped
around those who fear God, to rescue them.
Taste and see that the Lord is good.
They are happy who seek refuge in God.

Psalm (33) 34: 6–9

Every morning moment
fresh
new
exciting
delightful
as the first
creation morning

Taste and see that the Lord is good.

LORD, YOU have been our refuge
from one generation to the next.

All our days pass away in your anger.
Our life is over like a sigh.
Our span is seventy years,
or eighty for those who are strong.

And most of these are emptiness and pain.
They pass swiftly and we are gone.
Who understands the power of your anger
and fears the strength of your fury?

Make us know the shortness of our life
that we may gain wisdom of heart.
Lord, relent! Is your anger for ever?
Show pity to your servants.

Psalm (89) 90: 1, 9–13

Prime
holy time

time out
of schedules
we build
to make us feel safe

time out
of timetables
we create
to keep us on track

time out
of routines
we impose
to give us the illusion of control

The rhythm of holy time
loosens the chains
that bind us
setting us free
bringing peace

Make us know the shortness of our life that we
may gain wisdom of heart.

WILL BLESS the Lord at all times,
God's praise always on my lips;
in the Lord my soul shall make its boast.
The humble shall hear and be glad.

Glorify the Lord with me.
Together let us praise God's name.
I sought the Lord and was heard;
from all my terrors set free.

Psalm (33) 34: 2–5

Stopping at terce
a discipline

bringing comfort
bringing support
helping us feel safe
giving us something to hold on to

as we freely shake off rules and regulations
leave behind scales and notes
move into the music
dive into the sea
sail across the lake
listen to our heart's cry
relax in the sound of silence
reach for divine freedom
and truth

In the Lord my soul shall make its boast.

VOICE I did not know said to me:
'I freed your shoulder from the burden;
your hands were freed from the load.
You called in distress and I saved you.

I answered, concealed in the storm cloud;
at the waters of Meribah I tested you.
Listen, my people, to my warning.
O Israel, if only you would heed!'

Psalm (80) 81: 7–9

Midday
enthusiasm flagging
crisis looming
dejection threatening
the challenges of the day overwhelming us

Sext
reminding us to
stop

calling us to
reflect
catch our breath
make peace
find joy
take rest
find strength
in the moment

**You called in distress and I saved you. I answered,
concealed in the storm cloud.**

HOSE WHO PUT their trust in the Lord
are like Mount Zion, that cannot be
shaken, that stands for ever.

Jerusalem! The mountains surround her,
so the Lord surrounds his people
both now and for ever.

Do good, Lord, to those who are good,
to the upright of heart;
but the crooked and those who do evil,
drive them away!

On Israel, peace!

Psalm (124) 125: 1–2, 4–5

Aspiring to good
we inspire others
to goodness

Aspired to good
we reject
competitiveness
prejudice
judgement
hypocrisy
cynicism
negativity
arrogance
closed-mindedness
aggression

71

Aspiring to good
we inspire others to
give
heal
forgive
with
tenderness
openness
affirmation
creativity
goodness

Do good, Lord, to those who are good.

OME IN; LET us bow and bend low;
let us kneel before the God who made us
for this is our God and we
the people who belong to his pasture,
the flock that is led by his hand.

O that today you would listen to God's voice!
'Harden not your hearts as at Meribah,
as on that day at Massah in the desert
when your ancestors put me to the test;
when they tried me, though they saw my work.'

Psalm (94) 95: 6–9

There is never a moment
that isn't an opportunity
to create something new

There is never a moment
when there isn't something
to let go

There is never a moment
that isn't an opportunity
to make space for the new
by letting go of the old

Let us kneel before the God who made us.

ou, O LORD, are my lamp,
my God who lightens my darkness.
With you I can break through any barrier,
with my God I can scale any wall.

Your ways, O God, are perfect;
your word, O Lord, is purest gold.
You indeed are the shield
of all who make you their refuge.

Psalm (17) 18: 29–31

The harvest of our lives
is already with us
we are blessed

Opening to the gifts of the day we
savour
relish
rest
rejoice
in what we have been given
announcing
our blessedness
the delicious fruits of the spirit

With my God I can scale any wall.

OW GREAT IS your name,
O Lord our God, through all the earth!

Your majesty is praised above the heavens;
on the lips of children and of babes
you found praise to foil your enemy,
to silence the foe and the rebel.

Psalm 8: 2–3

You, God of all the earth
God of
Abraham and Sarah
Isaac and Rebecca
Jacob and Rachel

are beyond categories
beyond masculine and feminine

are eternally unnamed
You are eternal mystery

How great is your name, O Lord our God,
through all the earth!

Y HEART IS ready, O God;
I will sing, sing your praise.
Awake, my soul;
awake, lyre and harp,
I will awake the dawn.

I will thank you, Lord, among the peoples,
among the nations I will praise you,
for your love reaches to the heavens
and your truth to the skies.
O God, arise above the heavens;
may your glory shine on earth!

Psalm (107) 108: 2–6

Waiting
watching
in the still, dark silence
not knowing

then just before sunrise
the world takes in a deep breath
birds awake
a crescendo of cacophonous twitters
salutes the day

dawn chorus
exhaling new life
echoing over the earth

**Awake, my soul; awake, lyre and harp, I will awake
the dawn.**

N THE MORNING, fill us with your love;
we shall exult and rejoice all our days.
Give us joy to balance our affliction
for the years when we knew misfortune.

Show forth your work to your servants;
let your glory shine on their children.
Let the favour of the Lord be upon us:
give success to the work of our hands.

Psalm (89) 90: 14–17

Prime
a prayer for courage

Courage
gift of the heart
opening us to
experience
accept
know our pain

The pain of life
experienced
accepted with courage
awakens our love
stirs our compassion
melts our hardness
frees our creativity
opens our mind
a gift of the heart

In the morning, fill us with your love.

I WAS THRUST down, thrust down and falling,
but the Lord was my helper.
The Lord is my strength and my song;
and has been my saviour.
There are shouts of joy and victory
in the tents of the just.

The Lord's right hand has triumphed;
God's right hand raised me.
The Lord's right hand has triumphed;
I shall not die, I shall live
and recount God's deeds.

Psalm (117) 118: 13–17

Stopping
at terce

an invitation
to listen
to the quiet voice within
the unheard voices around

voices speaking to us
teaching us
reminding us
who it is
we are
where it is
we are going

The Lord is my strength and my song.

AY YOUR HAND be on the one
you have chosen,
the one you have given your strength.
and we shall never forsake you again;
give us life that we may call upon your name.

God of hosts, bring us back;
let your face shine on us and we shall be saved.

Psalm (79) 80: 18–20

The chant of sext
time to

sift
the viable from the moribund

separate
the gold from the dross

reflect
on what we need
can let go
gather together
before moving on

**God of hosts, bring us back; let your face shine on
us and we shall be saved.**

HEN THE LORD delivered Zion
from bondage,
it seemed like a dream.
Then was our mouth filled with laughter,
on our lips there were songs.

The heathens themselves said: 'What marvels
the Lord worked for them!'
What marvels the Lord worked for us!
Indeed we were glad.

Psalm (125) 126: 1–3

Afternoon
naming
claiming
our gifts
our blessings

giving thanks
for what is good
in ourselves
in others
sharing with gladness
the marvels of our day

Realising our potential
our gifts shine out
as blessings

**What marvels the Lord worked for us! Indeed we
were glad.**

AY THE LORD answer in time of trial;
may the name of Jacob's God protect you.

May God send you help from the shrine
and give you support from Zion;
remember all your offerings
and receive your sacrifice with favour.

May God give you your heart's desire
and fulfil every one of your plans.
May we ring out our joy at your victory
and rejoice in the name of our God.
May the Lord grant all your prayers.

Psalm (19) 20: 2–6

Evening time
a reminder
that the darkness of negativity
is always
lurking
watching
waiting
trying to take hold

Evening time
negativity
faced
acknowledged
confronted
named

claimed
frees us
to let it go

May God give you your heart's desire and fulfil
every one of your plans.

ROM ON HIGH you reached down
and seized me;
you drew me out of the mighty waters.
You snatched me from my powerful foe,
from my enemies whose strength I could not match.

They assailed me in the day of my misfortune,
but you, Lord, were my support.
You brought me forth into freedom,
you saved me because you loved me.

Psalm (17) 18: 17–20

Compline
returning us
to ourselves
as we enter the night

drawing us
into the mystery of night
as we gather our day
offering it back to God
in gratitude

**You brought me forth into freedom, you saved me
because you loved me.**

OUR EYES SAW all my actions,
they were all of them written in your book;
every one of my days was decreed
before one of them came into being.

To me, how mysterious your thoughts,
the sum of them not to be numbered!
If I count them, they are more than the sand;
to finish, I must be eternal, like you.

Psalm (138) 139: 16–18

God of our life
seeking you with our mind
you slip our grasp
thinking we understand you
you change
believing we see you
you move ahead
seeking you in our heart
you reveal yourself to us
in truth
in the acceptance of the mystery
of your unknowableness

**How mysterious your thoughts, the sum of them not
to be numbered!**

T HE HEAVENS proclaim the glory of God,
and the firmament shows forth the work
of God's hands.
Day unto day takes up the story
and night unto night makes known the message.

No speech, no word, no voice is heard
yet their span extends through all the earth,
their words to the utmost bounds of the world.

Psalm (18) 19: 2–5

Creation
beginning time
before time
in time
all time

Creation
ongoing story
new beginnings
nothing complete

Creation
arising out of emptiness
taking form
returning again to emptiness
in a ceaseless rhythm
of new beginnings

The heavens proclaim the glory of God.

OD WILL CONCEAL you with his pinions,
and under his wings you will find refuge.

You will not fear the terror of the night
nor the arrow that flies by day,
nor the plague that prowls in the darkness
nor the scourge that lays waste at noon.

A thousand may fall at your side,
ten thousand fall at your right,
you, it will never approach;
God's faithfulness is buckler and shield.

Your eyes have only to look
to see how the wicked are repaid,
you who have said; 'Lord, my refuge!'
and have made the Most High your dwelling.

Psalm (90) 91: 4–9

Prime
pacing ourselves
taking time to be still
praying
meditating
listening to music

restores our balance
settles us down
allows us to flow
with a natural rhythm
with new belonging

our restless hearts
finding refuge
in the embrace of quiet

God will conceal you with his pinions, and under his wings you will find refuge.

HEY ARE HAPPY, who dwell in your house,
for ever singing your praise.
They are happy, whose strength is in you,
in whose hearts are the roads to Zion.

Psalm (83) 84: 5–6

Journeying outward
interesting
engaging
challenging
never fully satisfying

Journeying inward
slow
painful
leading to our heart's desire
discovering
our true selves

a place
of joy
of peace
of hope
of love

Two journeys
becoming one
blessings
peace

They are happy, who dwell in your house.

EMEMBER YOUR WORD to your servant
by which you gave me hope.
This is my comfort in sorrow:
that your promise gives me life.
Though the proud may utterly deride me
I keep to your law.

Psalm (118) 119: 49–51

Noontime
making space
resting
in the moment
remembering
the preciousness of life

Taking time
relishing life
with joy
with wonder
remembering
to give thanks

Your promise gives me life.

LET THERE be rejoicing and gladness
for all who seek you.
Let them ever say: 'The Lord is great',
who love your saving help.

As for me, wretched and poor,
the Lord thinks of me.
You are my rescuer, my help,
O God, do not delay.

Psalm (39) 40: 17–18

The world buzzing
with voices of
aggression
fear
doubt
criticism

Taking time in the afternoon
listening to our inner voice
in silence
in solitude
in peace
listening to our heart's voice
drawn into wisdom

Taking time to be
at nones

**O let there be rejoicing and gladness for all who
seek you.**

AM SURE now that the Lord
will give victory to his anointed,
will reply from his holy heaven
with a mighty victorious hand.

Some trust in chariots or horses,
but we in the name of the Lord.
They will collapse and fall,
but we shall hold and stand firm.

Give victory to the king, O Lord,
give answer on the day we call.

Psalm (19) 20: 7–10

Giving ourselves
to the process of the day
not controlled by success
or productivity
we come to live peacefully
with creative tension
centring ourselves within our day
enjoying what we do
for its own sake
relaxing in its fullness
as freely we let it go

Give answer on the day we call.

COME, BLESS the Lord,
all you who serve the Lord,
who stand in the house of the Lord,
in the courts of the house of our God.

Lift up your hands to the holy place
And bless the Lord through the night.
May the Lord bless you from Zion,
God who made both heaven and earth.

Psalm (133) 134: 1–3

Compline
recognising the universal rhythms
of day and night
sunsets and moon rises
great movements of seas and stars
seasons and natural cycles

Pondering in our hearts
creation's story
surrendering to the rhythms of
day and night
we savour the secrets of the day

Bless the Lord through the night.

Week Two

LORD, YOU search me and you know me,
you know my resting and my rising,
you discern my purpose from afar.
You mark when I walk or lie down,
all my ways lie open to you.

Before ever a word is on my tongue
you know it, O Lord, through and through.
Behind and before you besiege me,
your hand ever laid upon me.
Too wonderful for me, this knowledge,
too high, beyond my reach.

Psalm (138) 139: 1–6

God
we can never have enough of you
because your beauty
love
goodness
energy
are infinite
beyond imagining

having enough of you
you would not be infinite
you would not be God

**Before ever a word is on my tongue you know it,
O Lord, through and through.**

THE GOD OF gods, the Lord,
has spoken and summoned the earth,
from the rising of the sun to its setting.
Out of Zion's perfect beauty God shines.

(Our God comes, and does not keep silence.)

'Listen, my people, I will speak;
Israel, I will testify against you,
for I am God, your God.'

Psalm (49) 50: 1–3, 7

Silence embraced
glimpses of truth and beauty
become visible

The wise composer
allows music
to crescendo
reach a climax
and then—
pause
a rest
silence
nothing

Listening to silence
we hear the music

I am God, your God.

HE LORD IS great and worthy of praise,
to be feared above all gods;
the gods of the heathens are naught.

It was the Lord who made the heavens,
his are majesty and honour and power
and splendour in the holy place.

Give the Lord, you families of peoples,
give the Lord glory and power;
give the Lord the glory of his name.

Psalm (95) 96: 4–8

The ever-changing circle of time
a living statement to the eternal

we think we have no time
we think we are running out of time
we think time is out of our control

Time is eternal
we have all the time
we need
always

all time is ours
NOW

The Lord is great and worthy of praise.

F THE LORD does not build the house,
in vain do its builders labour;
if the Lord does not watch over the city,
in vain do the watchers keep vigil.

In vain is your earlier rising,
your going later to rest,
you who toil for the bread you eat,
when God pours gifts on the beloved while they slumber.

Psalm (126) 127: 1–2

Our world full of beauty
often hidden, abused
tiny
fragile

needing to be
supported
protected
acknowledged
appreciated
realised
loved into being

Our world full of beauty
stopping
we find it
finding
we recognise it

recognising
we embrace it
embracing
we love it into being

If the Lord does not build the house, in vain do its
builders labour.

HAVE CHOSEN the way of truth
with your decrees before me.
I bind myself to do your will;
Lord, do not disappoint me.
I will run the way of your commands;
you give freedom to my heart.

Psalm (118) 119: 30–32

Sabbath
a space
a time

saying yes
to the sacred

Sabbath
a joy
a rest

never a burden
never a chore

You give freedom to my heart.

IN THE scroll of the book it stands written
that I should do your will.
My God, I delight in your law
in the depths of my heart.

Your justice I have proclaimed
in the great assembly.
My lips I have not sealed;
you know it, O Lord.

Psalm (39) 40: 9–10

Nones
as shadows lengthen
time fades
day declines

Stopping
we notice how our attitudes
shaped our day

attitudes
developing our false self
limited
constricted
stilted
unfree

attitudes
delighting in our true self
expanded

unconditioned
fresh
forever free

we ask forgiveness
we give thanks

My God I delight in your law.

THE LORD IS king, with majesty enrobed;
the Lord is robed with might,
and girded round with power.

The world you made firm, not to be moved;
your throne has stood firm from of old.
From all eternity, O Lord, you are.

The waters have lifted up, O Lord,
the waters have lifted up their voice,
the waters have lifted up their thunder.

Greater than the roar of mighty waters,
more glorious than the surgings of the sea,
the Lord is glorious on high.

Truly your decrees are to be trusted.
Holiness is fitting to your house,
O Lord, until the end of time.

Psalm (92) 93: 1–5

No one lives by chance
everyone, everything has a purpose
a part to play
in the grand design
that is creation

Creation
a vast and living enterprise

every human, every tree, every organism
necessary for its completion

Being alive is sufficient proof
that we are all essential
to all creation
to all time
time to give thanks

From all eternity, O Lord, you are.

HESE THINGS WILL I remember
as I pour out my soul:
how I would lead the rejoicing crowd
into the house of God,
amid cries of gladness and thanksgiving,
the throng wild with joy.

Why are you cast down, my soul,
why groan within me?
Hope in God; I will praise yet again,
my saviour my God.

Psalm (41) 42: 5–6

Compline
completing the circle of day
mirroring the flow of life

letting go
of the mechanical forces
ruling our lives

reminding us to pace ourselves
according to the rhythms of
day and night
time and tide
our heartbeat
eternity

Hope in God.

Y SOUL IS waiting for the Lord.
I count on God's word.
My soul is longing for the Lord
more than those who watch for daybreak.
(Let the watchers count on daybreak
and Israel on the Lord.)

Psalm (129) 130: 5–7

Waiting
in the darkness of
blindness
helplessness
failure
despair

calls forth
faith
trust
yearning
longing
a letting go
as we await
God's coming
as light of morning

My soul is waiting for the Lord.

OD, WE PONDER your love
within your temple.
Your praise, O God, like your name
reaches the end of the earth.

With justice your right hand is filled.
Mount Zion rejoices;
the people of Judah rejoice
at the sight of your judgements.

Walk through Zion, walk all round it;
count the number of its towers.
Review all its ramparts,
examine its castles.

That you may tell the next generation
that such is our God,
our God for ever and ever
will always lead us.

Psalm (47) 48: 10–15

Creatures of the earth
born to live in rhythm with nature
rise with the sun
sleep with the dark
work in light

Most of us
rise to an alarm sound

move through our day
to the rhythm of timetables
caught up in the need to do
what we think needs doing
lie down again
with an alarm set
ready to start off another day's
unnatural rhythms

Our God for ever and ever will always lead us.

LESS YOUR SERVANT and I shall live
and obey your word.
Open my eyes that I may see
the wonders of your law.
I am a pilgrim on the earth;
show me your commands.
My soul is ever consumed
as I long for your decrees.

Your will is my delight;
your statutes are my counsellors.

Psalm (118) 119: 17–20, 24

This day
sets before us
opportunities to
accept
discover
affirm
delight
in the
uniqueness
giftedness
that is ours

This day
sets before us
the freedom to

PRIME MONDAY

accept
affirm
delight
in the
unique beauty
of all life

Open my eyes that I may see the wonders of your
law.

T THE RISING of the sun they steal away
and go to rest in their dens.
People go out to work,
to labour till evening falls.

How many are your works, O Lord!
In wisdom you have made them all.
The earth is full of your riches.

Psalm (103) 104: 22–24

Children delighting in bog
in swampy lands
where large water pools form

Children splashing through pools
lying on their bellies
silently watching muddy waters
slowly settle

Troubled waters are muddy

embracing muddiness
waiting
watching
refraining from
stirring
disturbing
brings an awesome stillness and clarity
when all is quiet

Children leaning over, seeing reflections
all those faces
in a pool of water

Children in their wisdom
teaching us
to watch and wait

Lord, the earth is full of your riches.

THE STONE WHICH the builders rejected
has become the corner stone.
This is the work of the Lord,
a marvel in our eyes.
This day was made by the Lord;
we rejoice and are glad.

Psalm (117) 118: 22–24

Sext
noontime
lunchtime
breaktime

nuns and monks
restoring body
replenishing energy
resting soul

A lighted candle
flowers on a table—
a meal becomes a feast
a celebration
alone
with others
rejoicing in the fruits of the earth
at noon

This day was made by the Lord.

ING PSALMS TO the Lord, you faithful ones,
give thanks to his holy name.
God's anger lasts a moment;
God's favour all through life.
At night there are tears, but joy comes with dawn.

I said to myself in my good fortune:
'Nothing will ever disturb me.'
Your favour had set me on a mountain fastness,
then you hid your face and I was put to confusion.

Psalm (29) 30: 5–8

Afternoon
so much
to give thanks for
be mindful of
alive to

what we have been given
received
learnt
what we have taken to heart
mind
body
during the day

Give thanks to his holy name.

I LOVE YOU, Lord, my strength,
my rock, my fortress, my saviour.
God, you are the rock where I take refuge;
my shield, my mighty help, my stronghold.
Lord, you are worthy of all praise,
when I call I am saved from my foes.

Psalm (17) 18: 2–4

Insight
the key
into full life
into our true selves

Insight
releases
all fear and threat
opens us to
honesty
integrity
justice
joy
transformation
enriching the day

You are the rock where I take refuge.

ou, Lord, are a shield about me,
my glory, who lifts up my head.
I cry aloud to you, Lord.
You answer from your holy mountain.

I lie down to rest and I sleep.
I wake, for you uphold me.
I will not fear even thousands of people
who are ranged on every side against me.

Arise, Lord; save me, my God,

Psalm 3: 4–8

At compline
we
put away the day
prepare to rest
aware there is a time for everything

a time to rest
as surely as there is
a time to work

You, Lord, are a shield about me.

LORD, MY heart is not proud
nor haughty my eyes.
I have not gone after things too great
nor marvels beyond me.

Truly I have set my soul
in silence and peace.
A weaned child on its mother's breast,
even so is my soul.

O Israel, hope in the Lord
both now and forever.

Psalm (130) 131: 1–3

Waiting
in faith
in silence
surrendering to
dark
nothingness
emptiness
powerlessness
we find
light in darkness
achievement in nothingness
fullness in emptiness
peace in silence
contentment in God

**A weaned child on its mother's breast, even so
is my soul.**

HE LORD'S IS the earth and its fullness,
the world and all its peoples.
It is God who set it on the seas;
who made it firm on the waters.

Who shall climb in the mountain of the Lord?
Who shall stand in God's holy place?
Those with clean hands and pure heart,
who desire not worthless things,
(who have not sworn so as to deceive their neighbour).

Psalm (23) 24: 1–4

*At dawn
before the clatter begins
in silence
in solitude
we hear a new day birthing
in us
around us*

*out of silence
the chant of lauds
gradually
opens our heart
quietens our mind
restores our senses
as we enter the day
with new awareness*

The Lord's is the earth and its fullness.

I T WAS YOUR hands that made me and
shaped me:
help me to learn your commands.
Your faithful will see me and rejoice
for I trust in your word.
Lord, I know that your decrees are right,
that you afflicted me justly.
Let your love be ready to console me
by your promise to your servant.
Let your love come and I shall live
for your law is my delight.

Psalm (118) 119: 73–77

A call into the mystery of who we are
a journey
of learning and discovery

learning
not to fear
uncertainty
vulnerability

discovering
inner strength
peace
energy
joy

in the morning

It was your hands that made me and shaped me.

OW MANY ARE your works, O Lord!
In wisdom you have made them all.
The earth is full of your riches.

There is the sea, vast and wide,
with its moving swarms past counting,
living things great and small.
The ships are moving there
and the monsters you made to play with.

All of these look to you
to give them their food in due season.
You give it, they gather it up;
you open your hand, they have their fill.

Psalm (103) 104: 24–28

Smell
source of
undiluted pleasure
joy unimagined
never merited
always available
smell of
freshly cut grass
ploughed fields
falling rain
morning dew
footed turf
mowed hay

salt water
fresh bread
high and low tides

Building our environment
filled with
petrol, nicotine, tar, grease, oil and cement
smells so offensive
we lose our sense of smell
pure gift
freely given to each of us
out of love
each day

The earth is full of your riches.

BRING AN offering and enter God's courts,
worship the Lord in the temple.
O earth, stand in fear of the Lord.

Proclaim to the nations: 'God is king.'
The world was made firm in its place;
God will judge the people in fairness.

Psalm (95) 96: 9–10

Taking time to
sit
bless
eat
nourish
digest

Creating space
for ourselves
for others
for all creation
A way to awareness
at midday

Bring an offering and enter God's courts.

OUT OF THE depths I cry to you, O Lord,
Lord, hear my voice!
O let your ears be attentive
to the voice of my pleading.

If you, O Lord, should mark our guilt,
Lord, who would survive?
But with you is found forgiveness:
for this we revere you.

Psalm (129) 130: 1–4

Forgiveness
the greatest of all giving

Forgiving
giving to all who have
injured
hurt
abandoned
supported
helped us

Forgiving
outgoing
heart-filled
not blaming
giving thanks

With you is found forgiveness.

OW GOOD AND how pleasant it is,
when people live in unity!

It is like precious oil upon the head,
running down upon the beard,
running down upon Aaron's beard,
upon the collar of his robes.

It is like the dew of Hermon which falls
on the heights of Zion.
For there the Lord gives blessing,
life for ever.

Psalm (132) 133: 1–3

A day lived in unity with nature
is a day lived as a circle
continuously flowing
in the eternal interconnectedness of creation

How good and how pleasant it is, when people
live in unity.

PON YOU NO evil shall fall,
no plague approach where you dwell.
For you God has commanded the angels,
to keep you in all your ways.

They shall bear you upon their hands
lest you strike your foot against a stone.
On the lion and the viper you will tread
and trample the young lion and the dragon.

You set your love on me so I will save you,
protect you for you know my name.
When you call I shall answer: 'I am with you.'
I will save you in distress and give you glory.

With length of days I will content you;
I shall let you see my saving power.

Psalm (90) 91: 10–16

Compline
a time to feel safe from
the difficulties of the day
the responsibilities of work
the speed of living
allowing ourselves be
restored
nourished
supported
sheltered
in the nest of the night

When you call I shall answer: 'I am with you.'

GOD, SAVE me by your name;
by your power, uphold my cause.
O God, hear my prayer,
listen to the words of my mouth.

For the proud have risen against me,
ruthless foes seek my life.
They have no regard for God.

But I have God for my help.
The Lord upholds my life.

Psalm (53) 54: 3–6

Nelson Mandela spent time
twenty-seven years
locked up
waiting
imprisoned in darkness
through his forties, fifties, sixties—
life wasted!

Waiting in darkness
he became light
shining
for his
people
party
country
world

I have God for my help.

LIFT UP my eyes to the mountains;
from where shall come my help?
My help shall come from the Lord
who made heaven and earth.

May God never allow you to stumble!
Let your guard not sleep.
Behold, neither sleeping nor slumbering,
Israel's guard.

The Lord is your guard and your shade;
and stands at your right.
By day the sun shall not smite you
nor the moon in the night.

The Lord will guard you from evil,
and will guard your soul.
The Lord will guard your going and coming
both now and for ever.

Psalm (120) 121: 1–8

Stopping
sitting still
letting thoughts go
moving gently
into ourselves
heart and soul
connecting with who we are

the emptiness of silence
becomes inexhaustibly full

activity
a mere trickle of its fullness

**I lift up my eyes to the mountains; from there
shall come my help.**

To you have I lifted up my eyes,
you who dwell in the heavens;
my eyes, like the eyes of slaves
on the hand of their lords.

Like the eyes of a servant
on the hand of her mistress,
so our eyes are on the Lord our God
till we are shown mercy.

Psalm (122) 123: 1–3

Our purpose this day
is not finding
security and certainty
it is discovering
the very best that is within us
our spirit
heart
creativity

Finding our spirit
following our heart
living creatively
we find
love
joy
freedom

To you, have I lifted up my eyes.

OME, RING OUT our joy to the Lord;
hail the rock who saves us.
Let us come before God, giving thanks,
with songs let us hail the Lord.

A mighty God is the Lord,
a great king above all gods,
In whose hands are the depths of the earth;
the heights of the mountains as well.
The sea belongs to God, who made it
and the dry land shaped by his hands.

Psalm (94) 95: 1–5

We give of our best
when we are
at our best

The more life exhausts
drains
stresses
the less we give

Unnatural rhythms
overshadow
eclipse
natural giftedness
uniqueness
bestness
our need for time
to celebrate

ourselves
each other
creation
our creator
each day

The natural rhythm of day
brings
joy
love
happiness
peace

Come, ring out our joy to the Lord.

BLESSED ARE you who fear the Lord
and walk in God's ways!

By the labour of your hands you shall eat.
You will be happy and prosper;
your wife like a fruitful vine
in the heart of your house;
your children like shoots of the olive,
around your table.

> *Psalm* (127) 128: 1–3

Food
—a form of meditation

Preparing
appreciating with love
smell
taste
colour
presentation
—a form of meditation

Receiving
remembering with love those who
prepared
cooked
served our food
—a form of meditation

By the labour of your hands you shall eat. You will
be happy and prosper.

LORD, REMEMBER David
and all the many hardships he endured,
the oath he swore to the Lord,
his vow to the Strong One of Jacob.

'I will not enter the house where I live
nor go to the bed where I rest.
I will give no sleep to my eyes,
to my eyelids I will give no slumber
till I find a place for the Lord,
a dwelling for the Strong One of Jacob.'

Psalm (131) 132: 1–5

Afternoon
lifting our hearts
in gratitude
for the gifts of the day

Forgiving
God's forgiveness
flowing through us into our world
wiping out offence

Forgiveness in the afternoon
bringing
peace at evening

I will give no sleep to my eyes, till I find a place for
the Lord.

IVE THANKS, AND acclaim God's name,
make known God's deeds among
the peoples.

O sing to the Lord, sing praise;
tell all his wonderful works!
Be proud of God's holy name,
let the hearts that seek the Lord rejoice.

Consider the Lord, who is strong;
constantly seek his face.
Remember the wonders of the Lord,
the miracles and judgements pronounced.

Psalm (104) 105: 1–5

Offering our day to God
morning
and evening

makes us less preoccupied
with doing
more aware of being
less preoccupied
with the decisions
more in tune with our deep desires
less attentive
to reason and logic
more attentive to our intuitions
less concerned
with 'why'

more open to
discovering the resources within ourselves

O sing to the Lord, sing praise; tell all his
wonderful works.

RESERVE ME, GOD, I take refuge in you.
I say to you Lord: 'You are my God.
My happiness lies in you alone.'

You have put into my heart a marvellous love
for the faithful ones who dwell in your land.
Those who choose other gods increase their sorrows.
Never will I offer their offerings of blood.
Never will I take their name upon my lips.

Psalm (15) 16: 1–4

Giving ourselves over to sleep
acknowledging
our need for rest
is accepting in part
our mortality

In sleep
we believe that simply being
is fruitful in itself

My happiness lies in you alone.

THE LORD IS in his holy temple,
the Lord, whose throne is in heaven;
whose eyes look down on the world;
whose gaze tests the people of the earth.

The Lord tests the just and the wicked,
and hates the lover of violence.

The Lord is just and loves justice;
the upright shall see God's face.

Psalm (10) 11: 4–5, 7

Darkness
faced alone

desolation
emptiness
loneliness
confusion
fear

Darkness
accepted
faced with
faith
hope
love

new life
born within us

bringing
peace
courage
vision

The Lord is just and loves justice; the upright
shall see God's face.

ND YOU, LITTLE child,
you shall be called Prophet of the Most
High, for you will go before the Lord
to prepare the way for him.
To give his people knowledge of salvation
through the forgiveness of their sins;
this by the tender mercy of our God
who from on high will bring the rising Sun to visit us,
to give light to those who live
in darkness and the shadow of death,
and to guide our feet
into the way of peace.

The Canticle of Zechariah Luke 1: 76–79

Dawn
cresting over the horizon
consecrates the day
a morning offering
beginning our day
consecrating us
anew

**Loving tenderness of our God, guide us into the
way of peace.**

LORD, YOU search me and you know me.

O search me, God, and know my heart.
O test me and know my thoughts.
See that I follow not the wrong path
and lead me in the path of life eternal.

Psalm (138) 139: 1, 23–24

We discover our uniqueness
in
taking risks
freeing our creativity
working with passion

Discovering our uniqueness
fills us with
energy
excitement
motivation

we find a joy
we didn't know we were looking for

O Lord, you search me and you know me.

ING A NEW song to the Lord
who has worked wonders;
whose right hand and holy arm
have brought salvation.

The Lord has made known salvation;
has shown justice to the nations;
has remembered truth and love
for the house of Israel.

All the ends of the earth have seen
the salvation of our God.
Shout to the Lord, all the earth,
ring out your joy.

Psalm (97) 98: 1–4

The more we bless
the more we are blessed

Our blessings
never run out
drawn
from a bottomless source
replenished
eternally

Shout to the Lord, all the earth, ring out your joy.

Y VOWS TO the Lord I will fulfil
before all the people.
O precious in the eyes of the Lord
is the death of the faithful.

Your servant, Lord, your servant am I;
you have loosened my bonds.
A thanksgiving sacrifice I make;
I will call on the Lord's name.

My vows to the Lord I will fulfil
before all the people,
in the courts of the house of the Lord,
in your midst, O Jerusalem.

Psalm (115) 116: 14–19

Eating and drinking
a political act
remembering
those who have
little food
too much food
waste food

Eating and drinking
connecting
to the whole world
as we
care for our bodies

to
live
work
help our neighbour
reverence the universe

A thanksgiving sacrifice I make; I will call on the Lord's name.

OR I KNOW the Lord is great,
that our Lord is high above all gods.
Whatever the Lord wills, the Lord does,
in heaven, on earth, in the seas.

God summons clouds from the ends of the earth;
makes lightening produce the rain;
and sends forth the wind from the storehouse.

Psalm (134) 135: 5–7

Nones
time of
forgiveness

Forgiveness
to fore give
before
during
after

Forgiveness
a taste of divine grace
pure gift

I know the Lord is great.

LESSED BE THE Lord, my rock,
who trains my arms for battle,
who prepares my hands for war.

God is my love, my fortress;
God is my stronghold, my saviour,
my shield, my place of refuge,
who brings peoples under my rule.

Lord, what are we that you care for us,
mere mortals, that you keep us in mind;
creatures, who are merely a breath
whose life fades like a shadow?

Psalm (143) 144: 1–4

Journeying towards the truth
living with
questions
uncertainty
ambiguity

secure in not knowing
never fully understanding
always seeking
never arriving

answers become questions
questions answers
a fulfilled day lived to the full

Lord, what are we that you care for us, mere
mortals, that you keep us in mind.

o you, O Lord, I call,
my rock, hear me.
If you do not heed I shall become
like those in the grave.

Hear the voice of my pleading
as I call for help,
as I lift up my hands in prayer
to your holy place.

Psalm (27) 28: 1–2

Surrendering to sleep
stepping out of the day
into night

setting aside our tasks
not because they are finished or accomplished
but because now it is time to rest

a time of
surrender
grace
sacredness
a holy time

Hear the voice of my pleading as I call for help.

COMPLINE THURSDAY

GOD, YOU are my God, for you I long;
for you my soul is thirsting.
My body pines for you
like a dry, weary land without water.
So I gaze on you in the sanctuary
to see your strength and your glory.

Psalm (62) 63: 2–3

In darkness
everything
appears meaningless
prayer valueless
God distant
people aloof
life empty
inspiration absent

Gazing on God
in the sanctuary of our heart
darkness
invites us
to know
without knowing anything

it is
in not knowing
that we know

**I gaze on you in the sanctuary to see your strength
and your glory.**

OU STRETCH OUT the heavens like a tent.
Above the rains you build your dwelling.
You make the clouds your chariot,
you walk on the wings of the wind;
you make the winds your messengers
and flashing fire your servants.

Psalm (103) 104: 3–4

Dawn
carrier of mystery
mystery of being
now
in time
between times
between dark and light

We live
now
not in the past, in the dark
not in the brightness
of light yet to come
only here
in this moment
experiencing
contentment
peace
oneness
the mystery of now

You stretch out the heavens like a tent.

A s FOR US, our days are like grass;
we flower like the flower of the field;
the wind blows and we are gone
and our place never sees us again.

But the love of the Lord is everlasting
upon those who fear the Lord.
God's justice reaches out to children's children
when they keep his covenant in truth,
when they keep his will in their mind.

Psalm (102) 103: 15–18

The purpose of this day is to
discover
accept
who we are
and what we are called to be

The purpose of this day is to
find the joy
we were born to know
the person we were born to be

The love of the Lord is everlasting.

SING PSALMS TO the Lord with the harp
with the sound of music.
With trumpets and the sound of the horn
acclaim the king, the Lord.

Let the sea and all within it, thunder;
the world, and all its peoples.
Let the rivers clap their hands
and the hills ring out their joy

at the presence of the Lord, who comes,
who comes to rule the earth.
God will rule the world with justice
and the peoples with fairness.

Psalm (97) 98: 5–9

Whatever we do
cook
clean
write
visit
walk
talk
listen
climb
rest
clap
dial
we do anyway

Doing whatever we do
lovingly
carefully
attentively
tenderly
with awareness
always brings inner peace

the message of mindfulness
the message of terce

Let the rivers clap their hands and the hills ring
out their joy.

ES, FROM THIS day forward
all generations will call me blessed,
for the Almighty has done great
things for me,
Holy is his name.

Luke 1: 48–49

Sext
a call to wholeness

Learning to
trust ourselves
follow our deepest desires
explore the recesses of our heart
we become whole

The Almighty has done great things for me.

APPY THOSE whose offence is forgiven,
whose sin is remitted.
O happy those to whom the Lord
imputes no guilt,
in whose spirit is no guile.

So let faithful people pray to you
in the time of need.
The floods of water may reach high
but they shall stand secure.
You are my hiding place, O Lord;
You save me from distress.
(You surround me with cries of deliverance.)

Psalm (31) 32: 1–2, 6–7

Walking with our woundedness
accepting our brokenness
forgiving
ourselves
others

free
empowered
without guile
without blame

the wisdom of maturity

Happy those in whose spirit is no guile.

ESCUE ME, LORD, from my enemies;
I have fled to you for refuge.
Teach me to do your will
for you, O Lord, are my God.
Let your good spirit guide me
in ways that are level and smooth.

For your name's sake, Lord, save my life;
in your justice save my soul from distress.
In your love make an end of my foes;
destroy all those who oppress me
for I am your servant, O Lord.

Psalm (142) 143: 9–12

Our spiritual journey
the greatest human adventure—

going beyond
certainties
knowledge
understanding
doubts
always journeying
towards an ever-unfolding truth

**Let your good spirit guide me in ways that are
level and smooth.**

ORD, WHO SHALL be admitted to your
tent and dwell on your holy mountain?

Those who walk without fault,
those who act with justice
and speak the truth from their hearts,
those who do not slander with their tongue,

those who do no wrong to their kindred,
who cast no slur on their neighbours,
who hold the godless in disdain,
but honour those who fear the Lord;

those who keep their word, come what may,
who take no interest on a loan
and accept no bribes against the innocent.
Such people will stand firm for ever.

Psalm (14) 15: 1–5

*The silence of the night
invites us to
detach ourselves from
possession of the day
entrusting it
entrusting ourselves
to the freedom of our God*

Who shall dwell on your holy mountain?

N MY BED I remember you.
On you I muse through the night
for you have been my help;
in the shadow of your wings I rejoice.
My soul clings to you;
your right hand holds me fast.

Psalm (62) 63: 7–9

Darkness
part of our way
into the gift
of life

accepting the way of darkness
we perceive light
we learn to know
beyond logic
beyond reason

a way of love

On my bed I remember you. On you I muse
through the night.

Y GOD'S WORD the heavens were made,
by the breath of his mouth all the stars.
God collects the waves of the ocean;
and stores up the depths of the sea.

Let all the earth fear the Lord,
all who live in the world stand in awe.
For God spoke; it came to be.
God commanded; it sprang into being.

Psalm (32) 33: 6–9

Dawn
aware of the rhythm
of giving and receiving
in each day

opening for us
a new consciousness
inviting us
to notice
reciprocate
each gesture
thought
touch
movement
creating life anew

energy replenished
in giving
in receiving

By your word the heavens were made.

OT TO US, Lord, not to us,
but to your name give the glory
for the sake of your love and your truth,
lest the heathen say: 'Where is their God?'

But our God is in the heavens;
whatever God wills, God does.
Their idols are silver and gold,
the work of human hands.

Psalm (113B) 115: 1–4

In detachment
from things
we are free from small-mindedness

In practising wakeful presence
we learn to take possession of ourselves

In letting go
we learn to live with ambiguity

In living with questions
we learn to wait for answers

**Not to us, Lord, not to us, but to your name give
the glory.**

OR YOU INDEED are the Lord
most high above all the earth,
exalted far above all spirits.

The Lord loves those who hate evil,
guards the souls of the saints,
and sets them free from the wicked.

Light shines forth for the just
and joy for the upright of heart.
Rejoice, you just, in the Lord;
give glory to God's holy name.

Psalm (96) 97: 9–12

Terce

stopping
opening ourselves to the day
blessing
appreciating
taking note of life's gift

stopping
looking inward
looking outward
celebrating life

stopping
we are present to the source of life
the immensity of the divine
the infinite touch of love

For you indeed are the Lord.

WILL THANK the Lord with all my heart
in the meeting of the just and their assembly.
Great are the works of the Lord,
to be pondered by all who love them.

Majestic and glorious God's work,
whose justice stands firm for ever.
God makes us remember these wonders.
The Lord is compassion and love.

God's works are justice and truth,
God's precepts are all of them sure,
standing firm for ever and ever;
they are made in uprightness and truth.

Psalm (110) 111: 2–4, 7–8

Wild flowers
caressing the earth with blessing
pulling them up
they grow again
in unexpected places
on pavements
rooftops
dying tree stumps
they find a way through

trampling them underfoot
they blossom and bless

The Lord is compassion and love.

OR GOD HAS said only one thing;
only two do I know:
that to God alone belongs power
and to you, Lord, love;
and that you repay us all
according to our deeds.

Psalm (61) 62: 12–13

Nones
evening drawing in
darkness falling
reminding
knowing
life
work
creation
will manage without us
until morning

inhaling
remembering
exhaling
letting go of the day

To God alone belongs power.

Y SONG IS of mercy and justice;
I sing to you, O Lord.
I will walk in the way of perfection.
O when, Lord, will you come?

I will walk with blameless heart
within my house;
I will not set before my eyes
whatever is base.

I will hate the ways of the crooked;
they shall not be my friends.
The false-hearted must keep far away;
the wicked I disown.

Psalm (100) 101: 1–4

Evening time
recovering our true self
exploring the
breadth
height
length
depth
of our inner being

taking us beyond our ego
connecting our individual life
with what lies beyond the self
journey of the soul and spirit

I will walk with blameless heart within my house.

ND SO MY heart rejoices, my soul is glad;
even my body shall rest in safety.
For you will not leave my soul
among the dead,
nor let your beloved know decay.

You will show me the path of life,
the fullness of joy in your presence,
at your right hand happiness for ever.

Psalm (15) 16: 9–11

Compline
calling us to
see with eyes of faith
leap in the dark
trust with the simplicity of a child
surrender to the protection of God
with thanksgiving

You will show me the path of life.

Week Three

OW LOVELY IS your dwelling place,
Lord, God of hosts.

My soul is longing and yearning,
is yearning for the courts of the Lord.
My heart and my soul ring out their joy
to God, the living God.

The sparrow herself finds a home
and the swallow a nest for her brood;
she lays her young by your altars,
Lord of hosts, my king and my God.

Psalm (83) 84: 2–4

Doubt
painful
embarrassing
confusing
making us feel failure
blocking our ability to pray

Faith
struggling
striving
persisting
light in crisis
bringing us home
to ourselves
as we welcome the day

God of hosts, my king and my God.

GOD, BE gracious and bless us
and let your face shed its light upon us.
So will your ways be known upon earth
and all nations learn your saving help.

Let the peoples praise you, O God;
let all the peoples praise you.

Let the nations be glad and exult
for you rule the world with justice.
With fairness you rule the peoples,
you guide the nations on earth.

Psalm (66) 67: 2–8

*Each new day
gifting us with
a tent of freedom
to proclaim the glory of God*

*a tent of freedom
to start anew
out of love
not necessity*

*a tent of freedom
through which everything is retrieved
even time
through which life passes*

*a divine freedom
empowering us*

graciously inviting
never forcing
respectfully calling us to
human freedom

Let all the people praise you.

F YOU TRUST in the Lord and do good,
then you will live in the land and be secure.
If you find your delight in the Lord,
he will grant your heart's desire.

Commit your life to the Lord,
be confident, and God will act,
so that your justice breaks forth like the light,
your cause like the noonday sun.

Be still before the Lord and wait in patience;
do not fret at those who prosper;
those who make evil plots
to bring down the needy and the poor.

Psalm (36) 37: 3–14

Patient waiting
in silence
teaches us to
believe in ourselves
hold nothing back
accomplish much
transform problems into possibilities

Be still before the Lord and wait in patience.

ET THE HEAVENS rejoice and earth be glad,
let the sea and all within it thunder praise,
let the land and all it bears rejoice,
all the trees of the wood shout for joy,

at the presence of the Lord who comes,
who comes to rule the earth;
comes with justice to rule the world,
and to judge the peoples with truth.

Psalm (95) 96: 11–13

Looking at a flower
knowing a flower
being a flower
becoming its root
stem
bud

Noticing the dew
being the dew
glistening in the silence
breathing freshness
nestling between blossoms

Becoming ourselves
here
now
today

growing
blossoming
blooming
blessing
radiating
peacefully
happily
joyfully
contentedly
satisfied with who we are

Let the heavens rejoice and the earth be glad.

LL THE PEOPLES, clap your hands,
cry to God with shouts of joy!
For the Lord, the Most High, we must fear,
great king over all the earth.

God goes up with shouts of joy;
the Lord goes up with trumpet blast.
Sing praise for God, sing praise,
sing praise to our king, sing praise.

God is king of all the earth,
sing praise with all your skill.
God is king over the nations;
God reigns enthroned in holiness.

Psalm (46) 47: 2–3, 6–9

Sabbath
rest
restoration
refreshment
breathing in
breathing out
thanksgiving
peace
joy

In keeping the Sabbath
we remember

everything
has its place
its time
we remember with
tenderness
love
wonder
joy
the beauty of our world
the beauty of our day

Cry to God with shouts of joy!

THIS IS MY resting-place for ever,
here I have chosen to live.

I will greatly bless her produce,
I will fill her poor with bread.
I will clothe her priests with salvation
and her faithful shall ring out their joy.

Psalm (131) 132: 14–16

Nones
stepping back

harvesting
the gifts of the day
reflecting on its fruits
giving thanks

knowing the difference
between
holding and grasping
needing and wanting

tasting with sweetness
peace
serenity
wellbeing
delight

This is my resting-place for ever, here I have
chosen to live.

CRY TO you, O Lord.
I have said: 'You are my refuge,
all I have in the land of the living.'
Listen, then, to my cry
for I am in the depths of distress.

Rescue me from those who pursue me
for they are stronger than I.
Bring my soul out of this prison
and then I shall praise your name.
Around me the just will assemble
because of your goodness to me.

Psalm (141) 142: 6–8

A day
with all its conflicts
inconsistencies
contradictions
messy
not neat

Integrating the different facets of our lives
we reduce the power of darkness over us
make the hostile hospitable
the strange familiar
find new meaning
we affirm life

**Listen, then, to my cry for I am in the depths
of distress.**

ou are no God who loves evil;
no sinner is your guest.
The boastful shall not stand their ground
before your face.

You hate all who do evil;
you destroy all who lie.
Deceitful and bloodthirsty people
are hateful to you, Lord.

But I through the greatness of your love
have access to your house.
I bow down before your holy temple,
filled with awe.

Lead me, Lord, in your justice,
because of those who lie in wait;
make clear your way before me.

Psalm 5: 5–9

Night-time
examining the day
being grateful
fore giving
confronting our fears with faith
looking back
leaning forward

**I bow down before your holy temple, filled
with awe.**

CALLED TO the Lord in my distress;
God answered and freed me.
The Lord is at my side; I do not fear.
What can mortals do against me?
The Lord is at my side as my helper;
I shall look down on my foes.

Psalm (117) 118: 5–7

Matins
reminding us
to trust the night
in its fearsomeness
in its awesomeness

In darkness light shines
knowing light
we come to know
darkness itself
is light

The Lord is at my side; I do not fear.

THE LAW OF the Lord is perfect,
it revives the soul.
The rule of the Lord is to be trusted,
it gives wisdom to the simple.

The precepts of the Lord are right,
they gladden the heart.
The commands of the Lord are clear,
they give light to the eyes.

The fear of the Lord is holy,
abiding for ever.
The decrees of the Lord are truth
and all of them just.

Psalm (18) 19: 8–10

In the silence and stillness of dawn
emptying ourselves of trivia
tuning into
our inner self
tuning into
God's dream in us
God's call in us

we notice people around us
the cry of their heart
reminding us
who they are
who we are
where we are going
how we journey together

Your decrees, O Lord, are just and all of them true.

HE LORD IS high yet looks on the lowly
and the haughty God knows from afar.
Though I walk in the midst of affliction
you give me life and frustrate my foes.

You stretch out your hand and save me,
your hand will do all things for me.
Your love, O Lord, is eternal,
discard not the work of your hands.

Psalm (137) 138: 6–8

Learning to accept and live with
polarities
tensions
paradoxes
contradictions
is the secret of wholeness

Accepting without understanding
honouring difference
finding unity in diversity
we move into the day

**Your love, O Lord, is eternal, discard not the work
of your hands.**

I WILL PRAISE you, Lord, with all my heart;
I will recount all your wonders.
I will rejoice in you and be glad,
and sing psalms to your name, O Most High.

But the Lord sits enthroned for ever.
The throne is set up for judgement.
God will judge the world with justice,
and will judge the peoples with truth.

Psalm 9: 2–3, 8–9

Born to
wonder
question
experience
explore

not special gifts
natural
being ourselves

toys
gadgets
equipments
technology
intended to
stimulate
entertain
teach
easily

quickly
hastily
denying the natural curiosity of childhood

Terce
a time to wonder

I will praise you, Lord, with all my heart.

APPY ARE THOSE who fear the Lord,
who take delight in all God's commands.
Their descendants shall be
powerful on the earth;
the children of the upright are blessed.

Wealth and riches are in their homes;
their justice stands firm for ever.
They are lights in the darkness for the upright;
they are generous, merciful and just.

Psalm (III) 112: 1–4

Living
by measurement
achievement
attainment
ambitions
goals and expectations
we easily forget the meaning of enough

Sext
a time
to remember
that enough is enough

a time
to know
when enough is enough

The children of the upright are blessed.

DELIVER US, O Lord, from our bondage
as streams in dry land.
Those who are sowing in tears
will sing when they reap.

They go out, they go out, full of tears,
carrying seed for the sowing;
they come back, they come back, full of song,
carrying their sheaves.

Psalm (125) 126: 4–5

Rushed and hurried
trading
happiness
for desire
mindfulness
for craving
generosity
for jealousy

in time
failing to distinguish one from the other
enslaved
in bondage

Nones
stopping to pray
surrendering our desires and cravings
taking time to relish our gifts
giving thanks

knowing
peace
joy
gratitude
love
freedom

Deliver us, O Lord, from our bondage.

UT AS FOR me, I trust in you, Lord;
I say: 'You are my God.
My life is in your hands, deliver me
from the hands of those who hate me.

Let your face shine on your servant.
Save me in your love.
Let me not be put to shame for I call you,
let the wicked be shamed!'

Psalm (30) 31: 15–18

In the peace of the evening
gathering together
our contradictory mixed-up day
accepting it for what it is
in all its imperfections

reconciling our mixed-up day
we increase the strength within us
moving into serenity

I trust in you, Lord; I say: 'You are my God.'

OW MANY, O Lord my God,
are the wonders and designs
that you have worked for us;
you have no equal.
Should I proclaim and speak of them,
they are more than I can tell!

You do not ask for sacrifice and offerings,
but an open ear.
You do not ask for holocaust and victim.
Instead, here am I.

Psalm (39) 40: 6–8

*Night-time
aware of our need for human intimacy
the ability and grace to show ourselves as we are
trusting we will be acceptable and accepted*

*In the sacredness of the night
we move beyond what is visible
into the core of our being
where we know we are
known completely
loved unconditionally
by our creator*

**How many, O Lord my God, are the wonders you
have worked for us.**

HAVE CALLED to you, Lord, hasten
to help me!
Hear my voice when I cry to you.
Let my prayer rise before you like incense,
the raising of my hands like an evening oblation.

Set, O Lord, a guard over my mouth;
keep watch, O Lord, at the door of my lips!
Do not turn my heart to things that are wrong,
to evil deeds with those who are sinners.

To you, Lord God, my eyes are turned,
in you I take refuge, spare my soul!
From the trap they have laid for me keep me safe,
keep me from the snare of those who do evil.

Psalm (140) 141: 1–4, 8–9

The silence of darkness
a time to read
the signs of our times
a time to listen
to the voices of the poor
a time to hear
in the depth of our hearts
a time to understand
what we are being called to
what is being asked of us
at this time
in this place

To you, Lord God, my eyes are turned.

RY OUT WITH joy to God all the earth,
O sing to the glory of his name
rendering glorious praise.
Say to God: 'How tremendous your deeds!

Because of the greatness of your strength
your enemies cringe before you.
Before you all the earth shall bow,
shall sing to you, sing to your name!'

Come and see the works of God,
tremendous deeds for the people.
God turned the sea into dry land,
they passed through the river dry-shod.

Psalm (65) 66: 1–6

Dawn
repetitious
inevitable
with awareness
always
full of surprises

Surprised by sunrise
it flows through our senses
transforming us with
lithesomeness
gracefulness
gratefulness

Surprised by sunrise
we take nothing for granted
we see and experience
God's miracles
everywhere

Cry out with joy to God all the earth.

I THANK YOU, Lord, with all my heart,
you have heard the words of my mouth.
In the presence of the angels I will bless you.
I will adore before your holy temple.

I thank you for your faithfulness and love
which excel all we ever knew of you.
On the day I called, you answered;
you increased the strength of my soul.

All the rulers on earth shall thank you
when they hear the words of your mouth.
They shall sing of the Lord's ways:
'How great is the glory of the Lord!'

Psalm (137) 138: 1–5

God in
each day
movement
gesture
turn and return
within and without

God in
clouds and sky
sun and moon
trees and flowers
creatures of sky and sea
lakes and rivers

mountains and hills
showers and rain
tears and laughter
night and day
darkness and light
breezes and wind
fire and water
air and earth

God in the
lure of invitation
joy of responding
searching
finding
remembering
accepting

God closer to us than ourselves

Thank you for your faithfulness and love.

GOD IS FOR us a refuge and strength,
a helper close at hand, in time of distress,
so we shall not fear though
the earth should rock,
though the mountains fall into the depths of the sea;
even though its waters rage and foam,
even though the mountains be shaken by its waves.

The Lord of hosts is with us;
the God of Jacob is our stronghold.

The waters of a river give joy to God's city,
the holy place where the Most High dwells.
God is within, it cannot be shaken;
God will help it at the dawning of the day.
Nations are in tumult, kingdoms are shaken;
God's voice roars forth, the earth shrinks away.

The Lord of hosts is with us;
the God of Jacob is our stronghold.

Psalm (45) 46: 2–8

Staying close
to affluence
wants increase
vessels enlarge
rarely full
never overflowing

Staying close
to the source of life
needs diminish
vessels reduce
always full
overflowing
with joy

The God of Jacob is our stronghold.

OOD PEOPLE TAKE pity and lend,
they conduct their affairs with honour.
The just will never waver,
they will be remembered for ever.

They have no fear of evil news;
with firm hearts they trust in the Lord.
With steadfast hearts they will not fear;
they will see the downfall of their foes.

Openhanded, they give to the poor;
their justice stands firm for ever.
Their heads will be raised in glory.

Psalm (III) 112: 5–9

Boredom
life force
blocked
enthusiasm
sapped
energy
dissipated
feelings
trapped
fears
preventing us from
experiencing joy

TUESDAY

SEXT

Facing our fears at midday
expressing our feelings
releasing our energy
feeling our enthusiasm
freeing our creativity
boredom dissipates
joy recovered

With firm hearts we trust in the Lord.

WILL GIVE you glory, O God my king,
I will bless your name for ever.

You are just in all your ways
and loving in all your deeds.
You are close to all who call you,
who call on you from their hearts.

You grant the desires of those who fear you,
you hear their cry and you save them.
Lord, you protect all who love you;
but the wicked you will utterly destroy;

Let me speak your praise, O Lord,
let all peoples bless your holy name
for ever, for ages unending.

Psalm (144) 145: 1, 17–21

Nones-time
withdrawing
with gratitude
counting our blessings
recognising enough
as enough
giving thanks for everything

I will bless your name for ever.

THE EYES OF the Lord are toward the just and his ears toward their appeal.

The Lord ransoms the souls of the faithful.
None who trust in God shall be condemned.

Psalm (33) 34: 16, 23

Within our day
we find what is sacred

Through our senses
the spirit speaks

Walking our path of life
we tread on holy ground

Ordinary events and objects
radiate the divine

Trust in God.

OU ARE KIND and full of compassion,
slow to anger, abounding in love.
How good you are, Lord, to all,
compassionate to all your creatures.

All your creatures shall thank you, O Lord,
and your friends shall repeat their blessing.
They shall speak of the glory of your reign
and declare your might, O God,

to make known to all your mighty deeds
and the glorious splendour of reign.
Yours is an everlasting kingdom;
your rule lasts from age to age.

Psalm (144) 145: 8–13

Looking deeply within
facing ourselves
our truth
our uniqueness
feelings
gifts and failings
knowing we are loved
loving and loveable
releases us from fear
heals us from our wounds
frees us to be ourselves
brings peace at night

**You are kind and full of compassion, slow to
anger, abounding in love.**

AVE MERCY ON me, God, have mercy
for in you my soul has taken refuge.
In the shadow of your wings I take refuge
till the storms of destruction pass by.

I call to you God the Most High,
to you who have always been my help.
May you send from heaven and save me
and shame those who assail me.

Psalm (56) 57: 2–4

God
always waiting to enlighten
all night long

Jacob struggled with the angel of darkness
with the presence of God
at dawn
struggle finished
Jacob's angel blessed him
with a disability

Entering into night
we too struggle with the angel of darkness
discover our true selves
at dawn
we are blessed
knowing our weakness is our strength

In the shadow of your wings I take refuge.

ING OUT YOUR joy to the Lord, O you just;
for praise is fitting for loyal hearts.

Give thanks to lord upon the harp,
with a ten-stringed lute play your songs.
Sing to the Lord a song that is new,
play loudly, with all your skill.

For the word of the Lord is faithful
and all his works done in truth.
The Lord loves justice right
and fills the earth with love.

Psalm (32) 33: 1–5

Mindfulness begets gratefulness

*Being mindful
giving thanks and praise
for what is given
we remember
what otherwise might go unnoticed*

*Giving thanks
an outward trust
we become
less concerned with what is missing
more focused on sharing
what will be given
this day*

Ring out your joy to the Lord.

OUR WILL IS wonderful indeed;
therefore I obey it.
The unfolding of your word gives light
and teaches the simple.
I open my mouth and I sigh
as I yearn for your commands.
Turn and show me your mercy;
show justice to your friends.
Let my steps be guided by your promise;
let no evil rule me.

Psalm (118) 119: 129–133

Living intentionally
demands discipline
heightens our consciousness
develops our sensitivity

As a musician, athlete, dancer
benefit from the discipline of routine
so we unfold and blossom with
vitality
joy
sensitivity
from a daily spiritual routine

Let my steps be guided by your promise.

BLESSED ARE THOSE whom you choose and call
to dwell in your courts.
We are filled with the blessings of your house,
of your holy temple.

You keep your pledge with wonders,
O God our saviour,
the hope of all the earth
and of far distant isles.

Psalm (64) 65: 5–6

Divine blessings
giving life
to our inner being
offering opportunities
to recognise our gifts
realise our potential
live our dreams

The best that we can be this day
is already within

We are filled with the blessings of your house.

ORD, LET YOUR love come upon me,
the saving help of your promise.
And I shall answer those who taunt me
for I trust in your word.
Do not take the word of truth from my mouth
for I trust in your decrees.
I shall keep your law always
for ever and ever.

Psalm (118) 119: 41–44

Simplicity
living close to the limits of our resources
with spontaneity and truthfulness
knowing our needs and our wants
being satisfied with enough
generous towards others

Simplicity
not equivocation
not manipulation
achieved by conscious and consistent
reflection and discernment
in honesty
with generosity
with grace

Sext
a call
to simplicity

Lord, I trust in your word.

 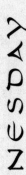

O GOD, HEAR my cry!
Listen to my prayer!
From the end of the earth I call;
my heart is faint.

On a rock too high for me to reach
set me on high,
O you who have been my refuge,
my tower against the foe.

Let me dwell in your tent for ever
and hide in the shelter of your wings.
For you, O God, hear my prayer,
grant me the heritage of those who fear you.

Psalm (60) 61: 2–6

Suffering humanity
alone
not alone
alone in this suffering
not alone in suffering

accepting
our aloneness
our finite selves
in the face of infinity
experiencing unity
in suffering
and in all things

From the end of the earth I call.

YES, IT was you who took me from the womb,
      entrusted me to my mother's breast.
To you I was committed from my birth,
from my mother's womb you have been my God.
Do not leave me alone in my distress;
come close, there is none else to help.

Psalm (21) 22: 10–12

One journey
two paths
the outer path
career
work
busyness
the inner path
heart space
hidden

An integrated day
travelling both paths
at one time

To you I was committed from my birth.

OW LONG, O Lord, will you forget me?
How long will you hide your face?
How long must I bear grief in my soul,
this sorrow in my heart day and night?
How long shall my enemy prevail?

Look at me, answer me, Lord my God!
Give light to my eyes lest I fall asleep in death,
lest my enemy say: 'I have prevailed.'
Lest my foes rejoice to see my fall.

As for me, I trust in your merciful love.
Let my heart rejoice in your saving help.
Let me sing to you, Lord, for your goodness to me,
sing psalms to your name, O Lord, Most High.

Psalm (12) 13: 2–7

*Our shadow
follows us
everywhere
every day*

*unrecognised
repressed
disowned
cast aside
it frightens
confronts
challenges us*

recognised
acknowledged
claimed
named
it illuminates
guides
comforts
brings peace
at night

Let me sing to you, Lord, for your goodness to me.

Y HEART IS ready, O God,
my heart is ready.
I will sing, I will sing your praise.
Awake, my soul;
awake, lyre and harp,
I will awake the dawn.

I will thank you, Lord, among the peoples,
among the nations I will praise you
for your love reaches to the heavens
and your truth to the skies.

O God, arise above the heavens;
may your glory shine on earth!

Psalm (56) 57: 8–12

Matins
a call to
to wakefulness
part of day
part of night

all day
calling us to wakefulness
a kind word
thought
disappointment
loss
mistake
new dream

vision
calling us to see and hear
with open hearts

My heart is ready, O God, my heart is ready.

LLELUIA!

Sing a new song to the Lord,
Sing praise in the assembly of the faithful.
Let Israel rejoice in its Maker,
let Zion's people exult in their king.
Let them praise God's name with dancing
and make music with timbrel and harp.

For the Lord takes delight in his people,
and crowns the poor with salvation.
Let the faithful rejoice in their glory,
shout for joy and take their rest.
Let the praise of God be on their lips
and a two-edged sword in their hand.

Psalm 149: 1–6

Recalling
the abundance of gifts
given to us
unmerited
gratuitously
we are moved to give thanks
at morning

Gratitude in itself brings happiness

In time
we learn

to give thanks
for everything
loss and gain
conflict and peace
sorrow and joy
sickness and health

Gratitude always brings happiness

Let the praise of God be on my lips.

IVE JUDGEMENT FOR me, O Lord,
for I walk the path of perfection.
I trust in the Lord; I have not wavered.

Examine me, Lord, and try me;
O test my heart and my mind,
for your love is before my eyes
and I walk according to your truth.

O Lord, I love the house where you dwell,
the place where your glory abides.

Psalm (25) 26: 1–3, 8

The way of truth
tests our heart
examines our motivation
relieves our suffering
challenges our commitment
brings loving perseverance
and always bears fruit

O Lord, I love the house where you dwell,
the place where your glory abides.

D O NOT BE afraid, for I have redeemed you;
I have called you by your name,
you are mine.
Should you pass through the sea, I will be with you;
or through rivers, they will not swallow you up.
Should you walk through fire, you will not be scorched
and the flames will not burn you.
For I am Yahweh, your God,
the Holy One of Israel, your saviour.

Isaiah 43 : 2–3

Terce
calling us to
healthy self-loving
balanced living

calling us to
depth
security
serenity
tenderness
honesty
trust
compassion

calling us to
be ourselves
every day

I have called you by your name, you are mine.

SHALL WALK in the path of freedom
for I seek your precepts.
I will speak of your will before the
powerful and not be abashed.
Your commands have been my delight;
these I have loved.
I will worship your commands and love them
and ponder your statutes.

Psalm (118) 119: 45–48

Doing
the energy
to move with focused attention
accomplish specific tasks
achieve goals

Being
the energy
to ponder
be centred
be fully present in the moment
with receptive awareness

Wholeness
balancing being and doing
the call of midday

I will worship your commands and love them and
ponder your statutes.

'HAT CAN BRING us happiness?' many say.
Lift up the light of your face on us, O Lord.

You have put into my heart a greater joy
than they have from abundance of corn and new wine.

I will lie down in peace and sleep comes at once
for you alone, Lord, make me dwell in safety.

Psalm 4: 7–9

Loneliness
a universal human condition

Loneliness
rejected
denied
avoided
bringing
alienation
isolation

Loneliness
faced
understood
accepted
bringing
health
happiness
peace

You alone, Lord, make me dwell in safety.

RAISE THE LORD from the earth,
sea creatures and all oceans,
fire and hail, snow and mist,
stormy winds that obey God's word;

all mountains and hills,
all fruit trees and cedars,
beasts, wild and tame,
reptiles and birds on the wing;

all earth's nations and peoples,
earth's leaders and rulers;
young men and maidens,
the old together with children.

Psalm 148: 7–12

Daylight fading
reflected
in shadows
changing shape and form

in a monastery garden
flowers
plants
prepare themselves for night
an enclave of nature

monks
praying
in the cloister

an enclave
at the heart of our world

Praise the Lord from the earth.

ORD, HEAR A cause that is just,
pay heed to my cry.
Turn your ear to my prayer,
no deceit is on my lips.

From you may my judgement come forth.
Your eyes discern the truth.

You search my heart, you visit me by night.
You test me and you find in me no wrong.
My words are not sinful like human words.

I kept from violence because of your word,
I kept my feet firmly in your paths;
There was no faltering in my steps.

Psalm (16) 17: 1–5

The shadow self
controls the self
as long as the self
rejects it
represses it

The shadow self
accepted
confronted
loved
forgiven
frees us into our true selves
to rest in peace

Turn your ear to my prayer.

N GOD ALONE be at rest, my soul;
from God comes my hope.
God alone is my rock, my stronghold,
my fortress; I stand firm.

In God is my safety and glory,
the rock of my strength.
Take refuge in God, all you people,
trusting always.
Pour out our hearts to the Lord
for God is our refuge.

Common folk are only a breath,
the great are an illusion.
Placed in the scales, they rise;
they weigh less than a breath.

Psalm (61) 62: 6–10

Rejecting
our aloneness
our emptiness
living
according to the expectations of others
we become
a collection of masks
defined roles
always looking for
a challenge
a crisis to solve

someone to heal
something
anything
filling our inner emptiness

Accepting our emptiness
embracing our aloneness
we grow and blossom
finding
the person we are called to be
—our true selves

God alone is my rock, my stronghold.

RAISE TO YOU, Lord, you have heard
my cry, my appeal.
You, Lord, are my strength and my shield;
in you my heart trusts.
I was helped, my heart rejoices
and I praise you with my song.

Lord, you are the strength of your people,
a fortress where your anointed finds refuge.
Save your people; bless Israel your heritage.
Be their shepherd and carry them for ever.

Psalm (27)28: 6–9

Today
greater than yesterday
when gratitude and praise envelop us

With gratitude and praise
we make peace with our world
with everything in our life
not excusing
ignoring
acknowledging all as part of us
we become whole

Lord, you are the strength of your people.

HAVE SOUGHT you with all my heart;
let me not stray from your commands.
I treasure your promise in my heart
lest I sin against you.
Blessed are you, O Lord;
teach me your statutes.
With my tongue I have recounted
the decrees of your lips.
I rejoiced to do your will
as though all riches were mine.
I will ponder all your precepts
and consider your paths.
I take delight in your statutes;
I will not forget your word.

Psalm (118) 119: 10–16

God beyond all understanding
bringing balance and harmony to
the boundless resources
the powerful energies
the store of strength
the endless potential
of our being

I treasure your promise in my heart.

GIVE EGYPT for your ransom,
and exchange Cush and Seba for you.
Because you are precious in my eyes,
because you are honoured and I love you.

Isaiah 43: 4

Living from our heart
a deeper way of knowing

Living from our heart
praising
with thanksgiving
with love

Living from our heart
giving
forgiving
healing

Living from our heart
wholeness
forgiveness
celebration

You are honoured and I love you.

BEND MY HEART to your will
and not to love of gain.
Keep my eyes from what is false;
by your word, give me life.
Keep the promise you have made
to the servant who fears you.
Keep me from the scorn I dread,
for your decrees are good.
See, I long for your precepts;
then in your justice, give me life.

Psalm (118) 119:36–40

Sext
calling us
to the simplicity
of a child
to live life in the moment
following our energies
connecting with our spirit
without distortion
or destruction

Keep my eyes from what is false.

LESSED BE THE Lord who has shown
me such a steadfast love
in a fortified city.

'I am far removed from your sight,'
I said in my alarm.
Yet you heard the voice of my plea
when I cried for help.

Love the Lord, all you saints.
The Lord guards the faithful
but in turn will repay to the full
those who act with pride.

Be strong, let your heart take courage,
all who hope in the Lord.

Psalm (30) 31: 22–5

Nones
twilight time
time between two worlds

Nones
frenzied world quietens
light recedes
darkness deepens
the unhurried pace
of the new world takes over

Nones
dusk
indistinct
forms and shapes
hazy
not defined
our world united
in formlessness
the twilight of day
the twilight of life

Be strong, let your heart take courage.

ᴇᴛ ᴛʜᴇᴍ ᴘʀᴀɪsᴇ the name of the Lord
who alone is exalted.
The splendour of God's name
reaches beyond heaven and earth.

God exalts the strength of the people,
is the praise of all the saints,
of the sons and daughters of Israel,
of the people to whom he comes close.

Psalm 148: 13–14

Time in the evening
connected with the earth
roots us in reality
relieves us from
anxieties
self-centredness
self-importance
seeing ourselves in the scheme of things

Time in the evening
connected with ourselves
with all creation
in touch with the
splendour of our being
splendour of the universe
a transforming experience

**The splendour of God's name reaches beyond
heaven and earth.**

LL THE EARTH shall remember and return to the Lord,
all families of the nations shall
bow down in awe;
for the kingdom is the Lord's, who is ruler of all.
They shall bow down in awe, all the mighty of the earth,
all who must die and go down to the dust.

My soul shall live for God and my children too shall serve.
They shall tell of the Lord to generations yet to come;
declare to those unborn, the faithfulness of God.
'These things the Lord has done.'

Psalm (21) 22: 28–32

Compline
a time to
forgive
radiate goodness
say good things
acknowledge the sacred
bless creation
call forth the best
in all things

**My soul shall tell of the Lord to generations
yet to come.**

WHEN YOU WENT forth, O God, at the
head of your people,
when you marched across the desert,
the earth trembled,
the heavens melted at the presence of God,
at the presence of God, Israel's God.

You poured down, O God, a generous rain,
when your people were starved you gave them new life.
It was there that your people found a home,
prepared in your goodness, O God, for the poor.

Psalm (67) 68: 8–11

Walking the road of life
we are called
to journey
into ourselves
into the vast interior of our psyche
of our soul
of our heart

At dawn
called
inward
deeper
further

we are called from
safety
comfort

knowing
into the unknown
into the dark

we are being challenged
to stay on the road
not to turn back
to trust our inner wisdom

believing
we will touch that sacred space
within

When you went forth, O God, at the head of your
people, your people found a home.

RY OUT with joy to the Lord, all the earth.
Serve the Lord with gladness.
Come before him, singing for joy.

Know that the Lord is God,
Our Maker, to whom we belong.
We are God's people, sheep of the flock.

Enter the gates with thanksgiving,
God's courts with songs of praise.
Give thanks to God and bless his name.

Indeed, how good is the Lord,
whose merciful love is eternal;
whose faithfulness lasts forever.

Psalm (99) 100: 1–5

God's joy is in us
given to us out of love
being born anew each day
in the richness of living
each moment
fully
always

Joy
cannot be organised
cannot be planned
we need only

desire it
seek it
it finds us

Joy transcending what we
think we can do
think we can be

Joy
always surprises

Serve the Lord with gladness.

HE LORD IS your guard and your shade;
and stands at your right.
By day the sun shall not smite you
nor the moon in the night.

The Lord will guard you from evil,
and will guard your soul.
The Lord will guard your going and coming
both now and for ever.

Psalm (120) 121: 5–8

Presence
a sacred experience
in stillness
a healing experience
in pain
a graced experience
in oneness
a joyful experience
in celebration
always there for us

O Lord, guard our going and coming both now
and for ever.

YOUR LOVE, LORD, reaches to heaven,
your truth to the skies.
Your justice is like God's mountain,
your judgements like the deep.

To mortals and beasts you give protection.
O Lord, how precious is your love.
My God, the children of the earth
find refuge in the shelter of your wings.

They feast on the riches of your house;
they drink from the stream of your delight.
In you is the source of life
and in your light we see light.

Psalm (35) 36: 6–10

Earth
strong, steady, serene, supportive

Air
light and free, without form

Fire
heat, bright, energetic

Water
flowing, swerving

Earth, air, fire and water
in us
around us
part of us
protecting us
bringing us to a place where we connect with
ourselves
each other
the universe

Your love, Lord, reaches to heaven.

I HAVE NO love for the half-hearted;
my love is for your law.
You are my shelter, my shield;
I hope in your word.
Leave me, you who do evil;
I will keep God's command.
If you uphold me by your promise I shall live;
let my hopes not be in vain.

Psalm (118) 119: 113–116

Bus, train delayed

reacting
shouting
fuming
leaving

accepting
staying
moving
quietly up the line

Aware or unaware
we create our own solutions
our own reality
by choice or by chance

Aware
we choose
our own reality

the desires of our heart
we choose
inner peace with joy and confidence

I hope in your word.

OD PROTECTS THE lives of the upright,
their heritage will last for ever.
They shall not be put to shame in evil days,
in time of famine their food shall not fail.

But all the wicked shall perish
and all the enemies of the Lord.
They are like the beauty of the meadows,
they shall vanish, they shall vanish like smoke.

The mouths of the just speak wisdom
and their lips say what is right;
the law of their God is in their heart,
their steps shall be saved from stumbling.

Psalm (36) 37: 18–20, 30–31

Living in fantasy
disconnected from truth
alienated from reality

False living
cut off from truth
disjointed
discomfited

Living in truth
healed
empowered

moving beyond alienation
anchored in reality
experiencing inner peace
we move through the day

The mouths of the just speak wisdom.

LLELUIA!
O give thanks to the Lord who is good,
whose love endures for ever.
Give thanks to the God of gods,
whose love endures for ever.
Give thanks to the Lord of lords,
whose love endures for ever;

who alone has wrought marvellous works,
whose love endures for ever;
whose wisdom it was made the skies,
whose love endures for ever;
who fixed the earth firmly on the seas,
whose love endures for ever.

Psalm (135) 136: 1–6

Inner peace
outcome of the day
we have lived

Listening with our heart
we come to know
colour
smell
touch
sound
of the day
and its message for us

**Give thanks to the God of gods, whose love endures
for ever.**

VESPERS ■ SATURDAY

Lord, PLEAD my cause against my foes;
fight those who fight me.
Take up your buckler and shield;
arise to help me.

Take up the javelin and the spear
against those who pursue me.
O Lord, say to my soul:
'I am your salvation.'

Let those who seek my life
be shamed and disgraced.
Let those who plan evil against me
be routed in confusion.

Let them be like chaff before the wind;
let the angel of the Lord scatter them.
let their path be slippery and dark;
let the angel of the Lord pursue them.

Psalm (34) 35: 1–6

To move beyond our fears
we must move into them
acknowledge
name
accept
confront
discuss
and talk them over until they

dissipate
disappear
lose their power over us

O Lord, plead my cause against my foes.

Week Four

S FOR ME, I will sing of your strength
and each morning acclaim your love
for you have been my stronghold,
a refuge in the day of my distress.

O my Strength, it is you to whom I turn,
for you, O God, are my stronghold,
the God who shows me love.

Psalm (58) 59: 17–18

Matins
a call
to journey into ourselves
a call
to wholeness
to know ourselves
to find our unknownness within
to reclaim that which is lost
to discover what is missing

a call
to journey into ourselves
a journey towards truth
knowing in a small way
who we are

the truth we think we know
we let go
to discover truth

O my Strength, it is you to whom I turn.

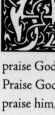

LLELUIA!

Praise the Lord from the heavens,
praise God in the heights.
Praise God, all you angels,
praise him, all you host.

Praise God, sun and moon,
praise him, shining stars.
Praise God, highest heavens
and the waters above the heavens.

Let them praise the name of the Lord.
The Lord commanded; they were made.
God fixed them forever,
gave a law which shall not pass away.

Psalm 148: 1–6

Children
illustrate the freedom of joy

Children do things for sheer joy
build houses and bridges
knock them down
build them up again
empty boxes
fill them
do things over and over again

Joy
is ours
when we do
what we really want to do
in freedom and integrity of heart

Let us praise the name of the Lord.

HEN I SEE the heavens,
the work of your hands,
the moon and the stars which you arranged,
what are we that you should keep us in mind,
mere mortals that you care for us?

Yet you have made us little less than gods;
and crowned us with glory and honour,
you gave us power over the work of your hands,
put all things under our feet.

All of them, sheep and cattle,
yes, even the savage beasts,
birds of the air, and fish
that make their way through the waters.

How great is your name, O Lord our God,
through all the earth!

Psalm 8: 4–10

Miracle of humanity
stemming from
'humus'
the earth
remembering
we are
dust and earth

Breath of God
enfolding

our nothingness
consecrating us
blessing us
reminding us
we are
human and divine

How great is your name, O Lord our God, through all the earth!

ORD, I LONG for your saving help
and your law is my delight.
Give life to my soul that I may praise you.
Let your decrees give me help.
I am lost like a sheep; seek your servant
for I remember your commands.

Psalm (118) 119: 174–176

Balancing
being and doing
life and work
brings harmony and contentment
to every experience
encourages us to
come alive to our true selves
fills us
with the life of the spirit
opens us to
receive what life is offering us NOW

Give life to my soul that I may praise you.

SEND FORTH your light and your truth;
let these be my guide.
Let them bring me to your holy mountain,
to the place where you dwell.

Psalm (42) 43: 3

Sext
a time to stop
reflect
accept what has been
live in the moment

a time to
prepare
commit to the future
with
confidence
strength
courage

O send forth your light and your truth; let these be
my guide.

WILL PRAISE you, Lord, you have
rescued me
and have not let my enemies rejoice
over me.

O Lord, I cried to you for help
and you, my God, have healed me.
O Lord, you have raised my soul from the dead,
restored me to life from those who sink into the grave.

Psalm (29) 30: 2–4

Nones
touching the depths
aware of our frailty
recognising our brokenness
connecting with the frailty of all humanity

Nones
accepting
all that divides
all that unifies
all that is broken
knowing peace

You have raised my soul from the dead.

IT WAS GOD who made the great lights,
whose love endures for ever;
the sun to rule in the day,
whose love endures for ever;
the moon and stars in the night,
whose love endures for ever.

Psalm (135) 136: 7–9

At the core of our being
we are all one
in the unity of things
we are drawn together
as we touch
and are touched by each other

we are a centre of gravity
in the heart of creation

God's love endures for ever.

LORD, LISTEN to my prayer
and let my cry for help reach you.
Do not hide your face from me
in the day of my distress.
Turn your ear towards me
and answer me quickly when I call.

For my days are vanishing like smoke,
my bones burn away like a fire.
My heart is withered like the grass.
I forget to eat my bread.
I cry with all my strength
and my skin clings to my bones.

Psalm (101) 102: 2–6

Night
time of
surrendering
resting
waiting
yielding
to the transforming power of sleep

Turn your ear towards me and answer me quickly
when I call.

EFORE THE MOUNTAINS were born
or the earth or the world brought forth,
you are God, without beginning or end.

You turn us back into dust
and say: 'Go back children of the earth.'
To your eyes a thousand years
are like yesterday, come and gone,
no more than a watch in the night.

You sweep us away like a dream,
like grass which springs up in the morning.
In the morning it springs up and flowers,
by evening it withers and fades.

Psalm (89) 90: 2–6

The journey towards wholeness
never complete
uncovering
reclaiming
gathering
integrating
discovering what is lost
losing what is found
a journey of light and darkness

You sweep us away like a dream, like grass which
springs up in the morning.

SING A new song to the Lord,
sing to the Lord all the earth.
O sing to the Lord, bless his name.

Proclaim God's help day by day,
tell among the nations his glory
and his wonders among all the peoples.

Psalm (95) 96: 1–3

Dawn
special moment of wonder
new moment
unmerited

All day every day
we have new moments of wonder
to be grateful for
fresh raindrops
wild flowers
sunshine
birds nesting
a card from a friend
conversations
a table tastefully arranged
an unexpected gift
a smile of welcome

Lauds
reminding us to
awaken to the wonders of dawn
open to the unexpected of the day
rejoice in each new moment

O sing to the Lord, bless his name.

YOU FOUNDED THE earth on its base,
to stand firm from age to age.
You wrapped it with the ocean like a cloak;
the waters stood higher than the mountains.

At your threat they took to flight;
at the voice of your thunder they fled.
They rose over the mountains and flowed down
to the place which you had appointed.
You set limits they might not pass
lest they return to cover the earth.

Psalm (103) 104: 5–9

Knowing
the happiness of
an integrated life
we bring
body, mind and spirit
into
what we do
who we are
living and loving
becoming one continuum
satisfying our deepest yearnings

You founded the earth on its base, to stand firm
from age to age.

ORD, HOW I love your law!
It is ever in my mind.
Your command makes me
wiser than my foes;
for it is mine for ever.
I have more insight than all who teach me
for I ponder your will.
I have more understanding than the old
for I keep your precepts.

Psalm (118) 119: 97–100

Awareness
giving perspective
to the journey of life

Journeying
with awareness
with attention
with mindfulness
each event unique
each step the first step
fulfilling

Journeying
without awareness
blinkered
hurrying onward to the end
shallow
empty
unfulfilled

The journey
sustains life
not the end

Lord how I love your law! It is ever in my mind.

ET THIS BE written for ages to come
that a people yet unborn may praise
the Lord;
for the Lord leaned down from the sanctuary on high,
and looked down from heaven to the earth
in order to hear the groans of the prisoners
and free those condemned to die.

Our descendants shall dwell untroubled
and our children endure before you
that the name of the Lord may be proclaimed in Zion
and God's praise in the heart of Jerusalem,
when peoples and kingdoms are gathered together
to pay their homage to the Lord.

Psalm (101) 102: 19–23

A piece of bread
sandwich
slice of fruit
cup of tea
become
a sacred meal
when taken quietly
mindfully
alone
with others

a moment of togetherness
a moment of sharing

a moment to give thanks
a celebration of fullness
the chant of sext

Let this be written for ages to come that a people
yet unborn may praise the Lord.

o you, LORD, I cried,
to my God I made appeal:
'What profit would my death be,
my going to the grave?
Can dust give you praise or proclaim your truth?'

The Lord listened and had pity.
The Lord came to my help.
For me you have changed my mourning into dancing,
you removed my sackcloth and clothed me with joy.
So my soul sings psalms to you unceasingly.
O Lord my God, I will thank you for ever.

Psalm (29) 30: 9–14

Nones
accepting
ourselves
others
allowing
our weaknesses
others' weaknesses
transform us
opening
to the next moment
with new awareness
new heart

I will thank you for ever.

Y SOUL, GIVE thanks to the Lord,
all my being, bless God's holy name.
My soul, give thanks to the Lord
and never forget all God's blessings.

It is God who forgives all your guilt,
who heals every one of your ills,
who redeems your life from the grave,
who crowns you with love and compassion,
who fills your life with good things,
renewing your youth like an eagle's.

Psalm (102) 103: 1–5

Vespers
in choir
monks and nuns singing chants

echoing
permeating
the visible
and invisible universe
past and present
every moment
every day

our thoughts, words, actions
echoing
connecting
transforming
influencing

impacting
permeating
finding their place
throughout the universe
past and present

All my being, bless God's holy name.

UT YOU, O Lord, will endure for ever
and your name from age to age.
You will arise and have mercy on Zion:
for this is the time to have mercy,
(yes, the time appointed has come)
for your servants love her very stones,
are moved with pity even for her dust.

The nations shall fear the name of the Lord
and all the earth's kings your glory,
when the Lord shall build up Zion again
and appear resplendent in glory.
The Lord will turn to the prayers of the helpless;
and will not despise their prayers.

Psalm (101) 102: 13–18

Surrender at compline
a form of prayer
accessible to us
even when prayer seems
empty of meaning
even when we have forgotten
how to pray

The Lord will turn to the prayers of the helpless.

LORD, YOUR strength gives joy to the king;
how your saving help makes him glad!
You have granted him his heart's desire;
you have not refused the prayer of my lips.

You came to meet him with the blessings of success;
you have set on his head a crown of pure gold.
He asked you for life and this you have given,
days that will last from age to age.

Your saving help has given him glory.
You have laid upon him majesty and splendour,
you have granted your blessings to him for ever.
You have made him rejoice with the joy of your presence.

Psalm (20) 21: 2–7

Our true self
open
receptive
limitless
boundless
unconditionally loved by God

**You have granted me my heart's desire, you have not
refused the prayer of my lips.**

G OD,
with you is Wisdom,
she who knows your works
and was present when you made the world;
she understands what is pleasant in your eyes
and what agrees with your commandments.
Despatch her from the holy heavens,
send her forth from your throne of glory
to help me and to toil with me
and teach me what is pleasing to you,
since she knows and understands everything.
She will guide me prudently in my undertakings
and protect me by her glory.

Canticle of Wisdom 9: 9–11

Life taken for granted
never knows joy

Joy is ours
in our wholehearted response to
opportunities
challenges
difficulties
meeting us throughout the day
in our wholehearted response to
the life we have
the person we are
this morning

With you is Wisdom.

LAUDS TUESDAY

YOU MAKE SPRINGS gush forth in the valleys;
they flow in between the hills.
They give drink to all the beasts of the field;
the wild asses quench their thirst.
On their banks dwell the birds of heaven;
from the branches they sing their song.

From your dwelling you water the hills;
earth drinks its fill of your gift.
You make the grass grow for the cattle
and the plants to serve our needs.

Psalm (103) 104: 10–14

Creation
reflected upon
prayed over
leads to gratitude
as we discover
a new power
within us
beyond us
present to us
nourishing us
serving our every need
calling us to new depths
each day

**You make the grass grow for the cattle and the
plants to serve our needs.**

OU HAVE PREPARED a banquet for me
in the sight of my foes.
My head you have anointed with oil;
my cup is overflowing.

Surely goodness and kindness shall follow me
all the days of my life.
In the Lord's own house shall I dwell
for ever and ever.

Psalm (22) 23: 5–6

O source of life
the more we
gather
store
hoard
put away
the less we receive

the more we
share
let go
give away
the more we receive

Inexhaustible source of life
you
nourish
refresh
cleanse

comfort
replenish
replace
restore
eternally

My cup is overflowing.

WILL PRAISE you, Lord my God,
with all my heart
and glorify your name forever;
for your love to me has been great,
you have saved me from the depths of the grave.

The proud have risen against me;
ruthless enemies seek my life;
to you they pay no heed.

But you, God of mercy and compassion,
slow to anger, O Lord,
abounding in love and truth,
turn and take pity on me.

Psalm (85) 86: 12–15

Conscious living
knowing inner freedom
working with dignity
without enslavement

Freedom
to take work up
put it down
to give thanks and praise
when the bell rings for sext
at midday

**I will praise you, Lord my God, with all my heart
and glorify your name forever.**

LLELUIA!

My soul, give praise to the Lord;
I will praise the Lord all my days,
make music to my God while I live.

Put no trust in the powerful,
mere mortals in whom there is no help.
Take their breath, they return to clay
and their plans that day come to nothing.

They are happy who are helped by Jacob's God,
whose hope is in the Lord their God,
who alone made heaven and earth,
the seas and all they contain.

Psalm (145) 146: 1–6

*Mid-afternoon
shadows gathering
a symbol of death*

*Nones
monks praying for a peaceful death
death a completion of life*

*Praying for a holy death
anticipating death with dignity
with peace
death a celebration
completion of life*

My soul, give praise to the Lord.

UT AS FOR me, I will always hope
and praise you more and more.
My lips will tell of your justice
and day by day of your help
(though I can never tell it all).

Lord, I will declare your mighty deeds,
proclaiming your justice, yours alone.
O God, you have taught me from my youth
and I proclaim your wonder still.

Psalm (70) 71: 14–17

Accepting the mystery of our being
not proving it
being it
we become
the self we were born with
the self we were born to be

O God, you have taught me from my youth.

HE LORD WILL not abandon his people
nor forsake his chosen heritage;
for judgement shall again be just
and all true hearts shall uphold it.

Who will stand up for me against the wicked?
Who will defend me from those who do evil?
If the Lord were not to help me,
I would soon go down into the silence.

When I think: 'I have lost my foothold';
your mercy, Lord, holds me up.
When cares increase in my heart
your consolation calms my soul.

Psalm (93) 94: 14–19

Compline
drawing us into
the movement of night
assisting us
to shift gear
enter more slowly
notice the greatness of God
as the sky changes
and night falls

**When cares increase in my heart your consolation
calms my soul.**

o you, O Lord, I lift up my soul.
My God, I trust you, let me
not be disappointed;
do not let my enemies triumph.
Those who hope in you shall not be disappointed,
but only those who wantonly break faith.

Lord, make me know your ways.
Lord, teach me your paths.
Make me walk in your truth, and teach me,
for you are God my saviour.

Psalm (24) 25: 1–5

Tuning into ourselves
into others
requires
inner calm
sharp concentration
deep intuition
an awareness
that remains quiet and clear
a perspective
extensive
deep
broad
focused

Tuning in
an invitation to

silence
stillness
enabling us to be
receptive
understanding
maybe even more confused
but in the end
more fruitful in whatever we do

Lord, make me know your ways.

T IS GOOD to give thanks to the Lord,
to make music to your name, O Most High,
to proclaim your love in the morning
and your truth in the watches of the night,
on the ten-stringed lyre and the lute,
with the murmuring sound of the harp.

Your deeds, O Lord, have made me glad;
for the work of your hands I shout with joy.
O Lord, how great are your works!
How deep are your designs!
The stupid cannot know this
and the foolish cannot understand.

Psalm (91) 92: 2–7

Early in the morning
the music of gratitude
rises easily in our heart
remembering
the many gifts
graces
chances
we have been given

Early in the morning
we see with great clarity
God's love
supporting
guiding

working
in us
with us
through us
the music of gratitude
available
all day
everyday
when we remember

Your deeds, O Lord, have made me glad.

URN YOUR EAR, O Lord, and give answer
for I am poor and needy.
Preserve my life, for I am faithful;
save the servant who trusts in you.

You are my God, have mercy on me, Lord,
for I cry to you all day long.
Give joy to your servant, O Lord,
for to you I lift up my soul.

Psalm (85) 86: 1–4

Humanity calling us
to the daily task of work

Calling us in our poverty and neediness
to make the world
a better place
a more just place
a meaningful place
a safe place
a call in history
a vocation in time
giving
and
receiving

To you, O Lord, I lift up my soul.

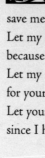

ORD, LET MY cry come before you:
teach me by your word.
Let my pleading come before you:
save me by your promise.
Let my lips proclaim your praise
because you teach me your statutes.
Let my tongue sing your promise
for your commands are just.
Let your hand be ready to help me,
since I have chosen your precepts.

Psalm 118 (119): 169–173

A cluttered mind
no space for thinking
an overburdened heart
no space for relationships

Emptying our minds
emptying our hearts
creates space for
safety
serenity
kindness
space for
listening
learning
knowing
as the hollow empty reed
leaves space for music

Teach me by your word.

REMEMBER YOUR MERCY, Lord,
and the love you have shown from old.
Do not remember the sins of my youth.
In your love remember me.

The Lord is good and upright;
showing the path to those who stray,
guiding the humble in the right path,
and teaching the way to the poor.

Psalm (24) 25: 6–9

Negativity
unacknowledged
unresolved
draining
attractive
alluring
addictive
crippling
controlling

Negativity
faced
named
claimed
awareness
peace
integrity
dignity

freedom
truth
happiness

Remember your mercy, Lord, and the love you
have shown from old.

ET OUR JOY then be in the Lord,
who rules forever in power,
whose eyes keep watch over nations;
let rebels not lift themselves up.

O peoples, bless our God;
let the voice of God's praise resound,
of the God who gave life to our souls
and kept our feet from stumbling.

Come and hear, all who fear God,
I will tell what God did for my soul;
to God I cried aloud,
with high praise ready on my tongue.

Psalm (65) 66: 7–9, 16–17

Life is a gift
everything
a unique expression of God's heart

Acknowledging God's gift
knowing it is our right
duty
privilege
to own
name
claim
who we are
what we do
how we do it

I will tell what God did for my soul.

HIS IS MY prayer to you,
my prayer for your favour.
In your great love, answer me, O God,
with your help that never fails;
rescue me from sinking in the mud,
save me from my foes.

Save me from the waters of the deep
lest the waves overwhelm me.
Do not let the deep engulf me
nor death close its mouth on me.

Lord, answer, for your love is kind;
in your compassion, turn towards me.
Do not hide your face from your servant;
answer quickly for I am in distress.
Come close to my soul and redeem me;
ransom me pressed by my foes.

Psalm (68) 69: 14–19

Being at home
where we
live
work
serve
recreate
pray
a blessing

a gift
a grace
an aspiration

a prayer
of petition
of gratitude

In your great love, answer me, O God.

THE LORD WILL bless those who fear him,
the little no less than the great;
to you may the Lord grant increase,
to you and all your children.

May you be blessed by the Lord,
the maker of heaven and earth.
The heavens belong to the Lord
but to us God has given the earth.

Psalm (113B) 115: 13–16

Fear
acknowledged
accepted
honoured
worked with
a way to inner peace

May you be blessed by the Lord, the maker of
heaven and earth.

WHERE CAN I go from your spirit,
or where can I flee from your face?
If I climb the heavens, you are there.
If I lie in the grave, you are there.

If I take the wings of the dawn
and dwell at the sea's furthest end,
even there your hand would lead me,
your right hand would hold me fast.

If I say: 'Let the darkness hide me
and the light around me be night',
even darkness is not dark for you
and the night is as clear as day.

Psalm (138) 139: 7–12

Stillness and silence
awaits us
everywhere
we don't have to travel from
the busyness of the city
the bustle of living

we find it
when we stop
when we notice
the petal of a flower
the cloud over the sun
the changing moon

the colours of the sea
the perfection of a newborn child
the blanket of snow
the leaves falling
birdsong
the countless wonders of day and night

O where can I go from your spirit, or where can I flee from your face?

LANTED IN THE house of the Lord
they will flourish in the courts of our God,
still bearing fruit when they are old,
still full of sap, still green,
to proclaim that the Lord is just.
My rock, in whom there is no wrong.

Psalm (92) 93: 14–16

With awareness
we arise today
like the morning sun
feeling safe
protected
watched over
cared for

we arise today
with courage
to ascend beyond the fray
regardless of difficulties
threats assailing us
criticisms meeting us
knowing
nothing can destroy
the gift of who we are

You are my rock, in whom there is no wrong.

AY THE GLORY of the Lord last for ever!
May the Lord rejoice in creation!
God looks on the earth and it trembles;
at God's touch, the mountains send forth smoke.
I will sing to the Lord all my life,
make music to my God while I live.
May my thoughts be pleasing to God.
I find my joy in the Lord.
Let sinners vanish from the earth
and the wicked exist no more.

Psalm (103) 104: 31–35

Sometimes
we are consumed by
the demands
of life
of work

At a deeper level they challenge us
to embrace our creaturehood
discover our heart's core
befriend our inner wisdom
recognise the music within
often taken for granted

**I will sing to the Lord all my life, make music to
my God while I live.**

ORD, YOU HAVE been good to your servant
according to your word.
    Teach me discernment and knowledge
for I trust in your commands.
Before I was afflicted I strayed
but now I keep your word.
You are good and your deeds are good;
teach me your statutes.
Though the proud smear me with lies
yet I keep your precepts.

Psalm (118) 119: 65–69

Facing the vulnerability of our humanness
the bedrock of truth

Exposing the fragility of our humanness
the way of truth

Reverencing the brokenness of our humanness
the mystery of truth

You are good and your deeds are good.

OD'S WAYS ARE steadfastness and truth
for those faithful to the covenant decrees.
Lord, for the sake of your name
forgive my guilt, for it is great.

Those who revere the Lord
will be shown the path they should choose.
Their souls will live in happiness
and their children shall possess the land.
The Lord's friendship is for the God-fearing;
and the covenant is revealed to them.

Psalm (24) 25: 10–14

Feeling unloved
rejected
unvalued
under attack
criticised
afraid
no good
not wanted
we find it hard to love

realising we are lovable
accepted
wanted
valued
loved
healed

loving ourselves
we love anew

Those who revere the Lord will be shown the path
they should choose.

LLELUIA!
God covers the heavens with clouds,
and prepares the rain for the earth;
making mountains sprout with grass
and with plants to serve our needs.
God provides the beasts with their food
and the young ravens when they cry.

Psalm (146) 147: 1, 8–9

*Each day
a unique gift
given
to be given*

*Gifts not given become burdens
harming
not freeing us
life taking
not life giving*

*Nones
giving thanks for all that is
given
taken
for all we have
given
received*

gifts of the day

Alleluia!

ISDOM IS BRIGHT, and does not grow dim,
by those who love her she is readily seen,
and found by those who look for her.
Quick to anticipate those who desire her,
she makes herself known to them.

Wisdom 6: 12–14

In the evening of our
day
work
life
we begin to know
truth
wisdom

In saying yes
accepting
embracing
loving
life
we discover who we are

Wisdom is found by those who look for her.

LLELUIA!

When Israel came forth from Egypt,
Jacob's family from an alien people,
Judah became the Lord's temple,
Israel became God's kingdom.

The sea fled at the sight,
the Jordan turned back on its course,
the mountains leapt like rams
and the hills like yearling sheep.

Why was it, sea, that you fled,
that you turned back, Jordan, on your course?
Mountains, that you leapt like rams;
hills, like yearling sheep?

Tremble, O earth, before the Lord,
in the presence of the God of Jacob,
who turns the rock into a pool
and flint into a spring of water.

Psalm (113A) 114: 1–8

Giving thanks for self
a step towards self-acceptance
accepting self
we learn to love ourselves
loving ourselves
we are healed

Tremble, O earth, before the Lord.

NSTRUCT ME, LORD, in your way;
on an even path lead me.
When they lie in ambush protect me
from my enemies' greed.
False witnesses rise against me,
breathing out fury.

I am sure I shall see the Lord's goodness
in the land of the living.
In the Lord, hold firm and take heart.
Hope in the Lord!

Psalm (26) 27: 11–14

In stillness and silence
we experience wisdom
challenging us
to listen
encouraging us
to take risks
loving us
into accepting ourselves

Wisdom waiting to be found
waiting for us
to discover
in stillness
in silence
the wonder of who we are

Instruct me, Lord, in your way.

GIVE THE Lord, you children of God,
give the Lord glory and power;
give the Lord the glory of his name.
Adore the Lord, resplendent and holy.

The Lord's voice resounding on the waters,
the Lord on immensity of waters;
the voice of the Lord, full of power,
the voice of the Lord, full of splendour.

The Lord will give strength to his people,
the Lord will bless his people with peace.

Psalm (28) 29: 1–4, 11

Morning
blessing us
with time and space
to be attentive
to all that is new

blessing us
with time and space to
look
listen
see
hear
become aware
of our world

blessing us
with time and space
to experience the divine
as sunlight
sheds its light on our world

blessing us
with time and space
to give thanks
go forth with strength
taking our part
in the divine design for the day

O Lord, give strength to your people and bless your people with peace.

LL THE NATIONS shall come to adore you
and glorify your name, O Lord,
for you are great and do marvellous deeds,
you who alone are God.

Show me, Lord, your way
so that I may walk in your truth.
Guide my heart to fear your name.

Psalm (85) 86: 9–11

Our unawakened mind
seeking happiness
searches
grasps
wants more
is restless
never satisfied
lost

Our awakened mind
seeking happiness
stops
reflects
ponders
knows
happiness is here
happiness is now

Show me, Lord, your way.

HEY ARE HAPPY whose life is blameless,
who follow God's law!
They are happy who do God's will,
seeking God with all their hearts,
who never do anything evil
but walk in God's ways.
You have laid down your precepts
to be obeyed with care.
May my footsteps be firm
to obey your statutes.

Psalm (118) 119: 1–5

Building walls
physical walls
psychological walls
cultural walls
spiritual walls
segregates and divides

As long as other people
are on their own side of the wall
seeing them
as walled-off categories
we are safe and secure
in our blindness

They are happy who walk in your ways.

THE LORD IS king, let earth rejoice,
let all the coastlands be glad.
Surrounded by cloud and darkness;
justice and right, God's throne.

A fire prepares the way;
it burns up foes on every side.
God's lightnings light up the world,
the earth trembles at the sight.

The mountains melt like wax
before the Lord of all the earth.
The skies proclaim God's justice;
all peoples see God's glory.

Let those who serve idols be ashamed,
those who boast of their worthless gods.
All you spirits, worship the Lord.

Psalm (96) 97: 1–7

Creation
always becoming
never complete
always being shaped
never static

Creation
moulding
fashioning
stripping

purifying
growing
blossoming
pruning
daring us
to become ourselves

**The mountains melt like wax before the Lord of
all the earth.**

I REJOICED WHEN I heard them say;
'Let us go to God's house.'
And now our feet are standing
within your gates, O Jerusalem.

Jerusalem is built as a city
strongly compact.
It is there that the tribes go up,
the tribes of the Lord.

For Israel's law it is,
there to praise the Lord's name.
There were set the thrones of judgement
of the house of David.

Psalm (121) 122: 1–5

Afternoon
being grateful
rejoicing
in life

being grateful
increasing awareness
perception
strength
courage
wholeness

being grateful
elevating the ordinary

extending boundaries
removing limits

being grateful
renewed
living with joy
living to the full

I rejoiced when I heard them say; 'Let us go to
God's house.'

EDEEM ME FROM those who oppress me
and I will keep your precepts.
Let your face shine on your servant
and teach me your decrees.
Tears stream from my eyes
because your law is disobeyed.

Psalm (118) 119: 134–137

Truth comes
in pairs of opposites

we are strong
when we embrace our weaknesses
we are teachers
when we can be taught
we enjoy others
when we enjoy ourselves
we are wise
when we accept our own foolishness
we find true laughter
when we laugh at ourselves

Teach me your decrees.

LLELUIA!

I love the Lord, for the Lord has heard
the cry of my appeal.
The Lord was attentive to me
on the day when I called.

They surround me, the snares of death,
with the anguish of the tomb;
they caught me, sorrow and distress.
I called on the Lord's name.

Psalm (114) 116: 1–4

Accepting our wounded nature
releases energy
focused on hurt
making it available
as a healing power
for ourselves
others
the universe

The Lord was attentive to me on the day
when I called.

HOSE WHO DWELL in the shelter of
the Most High
and abide in the shade of the Almighty
say to the Lord: 'My refuge,
my stronghold, my God in whom I trust!'

It is God who will free you from the snare
of the fowler who seeks to destroy you;
God will conceal you with his pinions,
and under his wings you will find refuge.

Psalm (90) 91: 1–4

When we are too busy
to be still
to be silent
to notice
we do not see what is around us
we do not hear what is being spoken

When we are too busy
our ears and eyes open
only to our projects and plans
we miss
the wonder of the moment
the wonder of our being
the wonder that leads to truth
the wonder of God

My refuge, my stronghold, my God in whom I trust!

HAPPY INDEED ARE those
who follow not the counsel of the wicked,
nor linger in the way of sinners
nor sit in the company of scorners,
but whose delight is the law of the Lord
and who ponder God's law day and night.

They are like the tree that is planted
beside the flowing waters,
that yields its fruit in due season
and whose leaves will never fade;
and all they do shall prosper.

Psalm 1: 1–3

As a tree
draws its sustenance
from the
sun
rain
soil
so too
we draw sustenance
from the source of all life

Like a tree
planted in good soil
by flowing waters
we too
rooted in love

delighting in God
yield fruit
in due season

Happy are those whose delight is in the
law of the Lord.

YOU HAVE GIVEN me a short span of days;
my life is as nothing in your sight.
A mere breath, the one who stood so firm;
a mere shadow, the one who passes by;
a mere breath, the hoarded riches,
and who will take them, no one knows.

In you rests all my hope.

Psalm (38) 39: 6–7, 8

Prime
challenging us
to be fully present
in life
in work
out of work
at home
out of home
wherever we are
now

Tomorrow
the enemy of today
we cannot be tomorrow
what we can be today

In you rests all my hope.

PURE HEART create for me, O God,
put a steadfast spirit within me.
Do not cast me away from your presence,
nor deprive me of your holy spirit.

Give me again the joy of your help;
with a spirit of fervour sustain me,
that I may teach transgressors your ways
and sinners may return to you.

Psalm (50) 51: 12–14

Faith
living with promise
with waiting
with darkness
with ambiguity
with uncertainty

Faith
gentle strength
without answers

Give me again the joy of your help.

 ow GRACIOUS IS the Lord, and just;
our God has compassion.
The Lord protects the simple hearts;
I was helpless so God saved me.

Turn back, my soul, to your rest
for the Lord has been good,
and has kept my soul from death,
(my eyes from tears),
my feet from stumbling.

I will walk in the presence of the Lord
in the land of the living.

Psalm (114) 116: 5–9

Sext
fallow time
resting
preparing
for the next time

Rest-time
bringing
vigour
nourishment
renewal
openness

bringing
readiness

344

to listen
to respond
a call from the spirit
to be

I will walk in the presence of the Lord in the land of the living.

GIVE THANKS to the Lord who is good;
whose love endures for ever.
Who can tell the Lord's mighty deeds?
Who can recount all God's praise?

They are happy who do what is right,
who at all times do what is just.
O Lord, remember me
out of the love that you have for your people.

Come to me, Lord, with your help
that I may see the joy of your chosen ones
and may rejoice in the gladness of your nation
and share the glory of your people.

Psalm (105) 106: 1–5

False humility
deluding us into
trying to be what we are not
consuming us
preventing us
from acknowledging
our gifts
the gift of others

True humility
feeling secure
in uncertainty
owning our gifts

recognising the gifts of others
giving thanks

O give thanks to the Lord who is good; whose
love endures forever.

LLELUIA!

Give thanks to the Lord who is good,
for God's love endures for ever.

Let the family of Israel say:
'God's love endures for ever.'
Let the family of Aaron say:
'God's love endures for ever.'
Let those who fear the Lord say:
'God's love endures for ever.'

Psalm (117) 118: 1–4

*Many of us become
what others tell us we are*

*Masculine
doing, active, rational, strong, organised,
serious, responsible, intellectual*

*Feminine
being, passive, intuitive, vulnerable,
spontaneous, spiritual, receptive, emotional*

*Listening to the small voice within
we discover the person we are called to be
in our being
in our doing
our delightful uniqueness*

Give thanks to the Lord who is good.

WILL BLESS you day after day
and praise your name for ever.
You are great, Lord, highly to be praised,
your greatness cannot be measured.

Age to age shall proclaim your works,
shall declare your mighty deeds,
shall speak of your splendour and glory,
tell the tale of your wonderful works.

Psalm (144)145: 2–5

Living in the moment
ensures we do not miss the present
or find it gone
before we have experienced it

ensures we do not find day
has passed us by
before we have fully lived it
helps us greet the night
with gratitude
helps us welcome death
when its moment comes

Age to age shall proclaim your works.

History of the
Canonical Hours

Chanting is not confined to the Christian tradition, but is part of all religious traditions: Buddhist, Hindu, Jewish, Islamic and others. At a certain pitch of religious experience, the heart just wants to sing and so it breaks into song.

The chanting of what is now known as the liturgy of hours, or the canonical hours, goes back over many centuries and is believed to derive from the Jewish practice of chanting the psalms. Its earliest forms can be traced to Palestine and Syria. The early Christian Church continued that tradition of communal chanting of psalms and prayers and, gradually, a common formula for this worship evolved into the canonical hours we have today.

In the beginning, there was a very strong oral tradition, with no written music. Some of the melodies, verses and refrains were well known by ordinary people as well as by people in religious life. Over the years, a whole repertoire of written music to accompany the psalms was composed. Gregory I, who was pope between AD 590 and 604, commanded that a way should be found to collect and preserve this sacred music, and he was responsible for reorganising the services and establishing choral schools and choirs in the churches. Around the same time, 1500 years ago, Saint Benedict founded the Benedictine order and the chants of the canonical hours are very much associated with the Benedictine rule.

In the Middle Ages, Gregorian chant, which was flourishing within the Holy Roman Empire, assumed what is today considered to be its traditional form, though later musical innovations developed. Over time, this form of singing became more complex and grew less popular amongst the ordinary people and became the preserve of professionals and monasteries.

In the 19th century, amid controversy about what the Gregorian chant should be, the Benedictine monks of Solesmes, in France, embarked on a century-long effort to restore the chant to its mediaeval form. Working with original manuscripts found all over Europe, they established the proper interpretation of hundreds of chants.

Now is the Time

Spiritual Reflections
Sister Stan

Now is the Time became an instant bestseller when it was first published, and in this expanded edition, which includes five new entries, Stan's message remains the same: we have the time, if we make the choice to take time . . .

Now is the Time is a book for everyone; young or old, male or female, for the converted or those who are irreligious or plain disaffected. Even people for whom a spiritual view of the world is a closed book should try opening this one.

Now is the Time looks beyond the boundaries of any one faith or church and draws on the great spiritual and philosophical traditions of east and west.

As Sister Stan focuses on a line of poetry from one of the world's great authors, an idea from a psychotherapist or philosopher, or a proverb from oriental wisdom, she weaves her own thoughts around them in a way that presents them afresh, and allows us to see them from a new perspective.

Now is the Time is an inspiring and thought-provoking work of vision.

9781848270633